REMOTE VIEWER

Graham Gussin

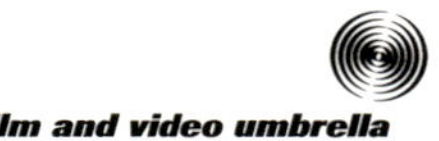

REMOTE VIEWER

Shot simultaneously in London and Iceland, September 2001

A remote viewer is a person trained to focus and hold his or her
sub-conscious mind on a distant target that is normally shielded by
time and space and record information about that distant person,
place or event

The artist made a trip to Askja in Iceland and during this time
a remote viewer attempted to trace/locate the artist without
having any prior knowledge of the subject or his whereabouts

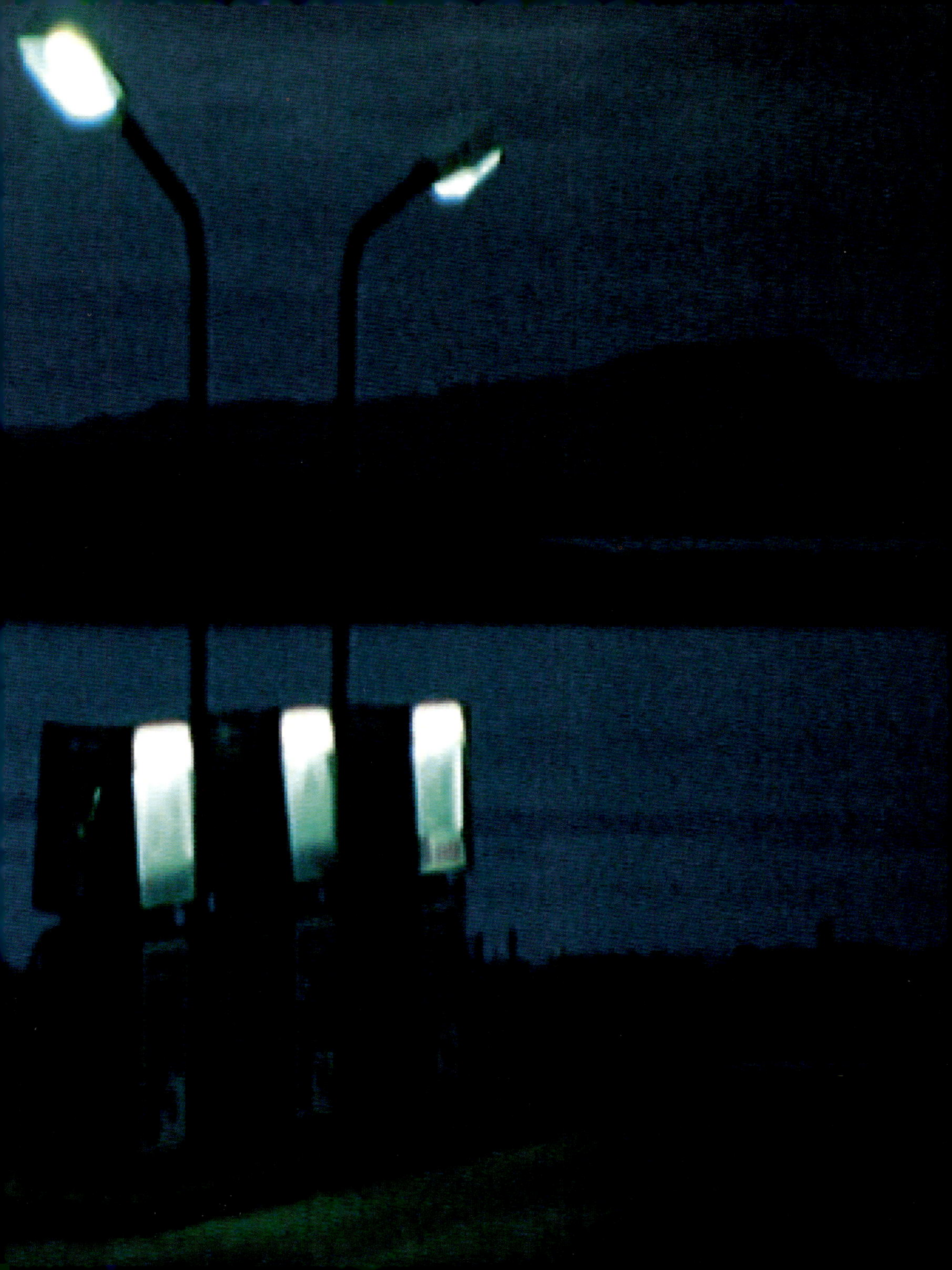

REMOTE VIEWING PROTOCOLS

Blackboard (initial target contact)

Spontaneous Ideograms (enabling sub-conscious reflex)

Matrix Protocol (sight, sound, temperature, texture, smell/taste)

Release Protocol (release from consciousness)

Cascade (uninterrupted visuals in the mind's eye)

graham gussin / askja / present time

KSGL — RRBV

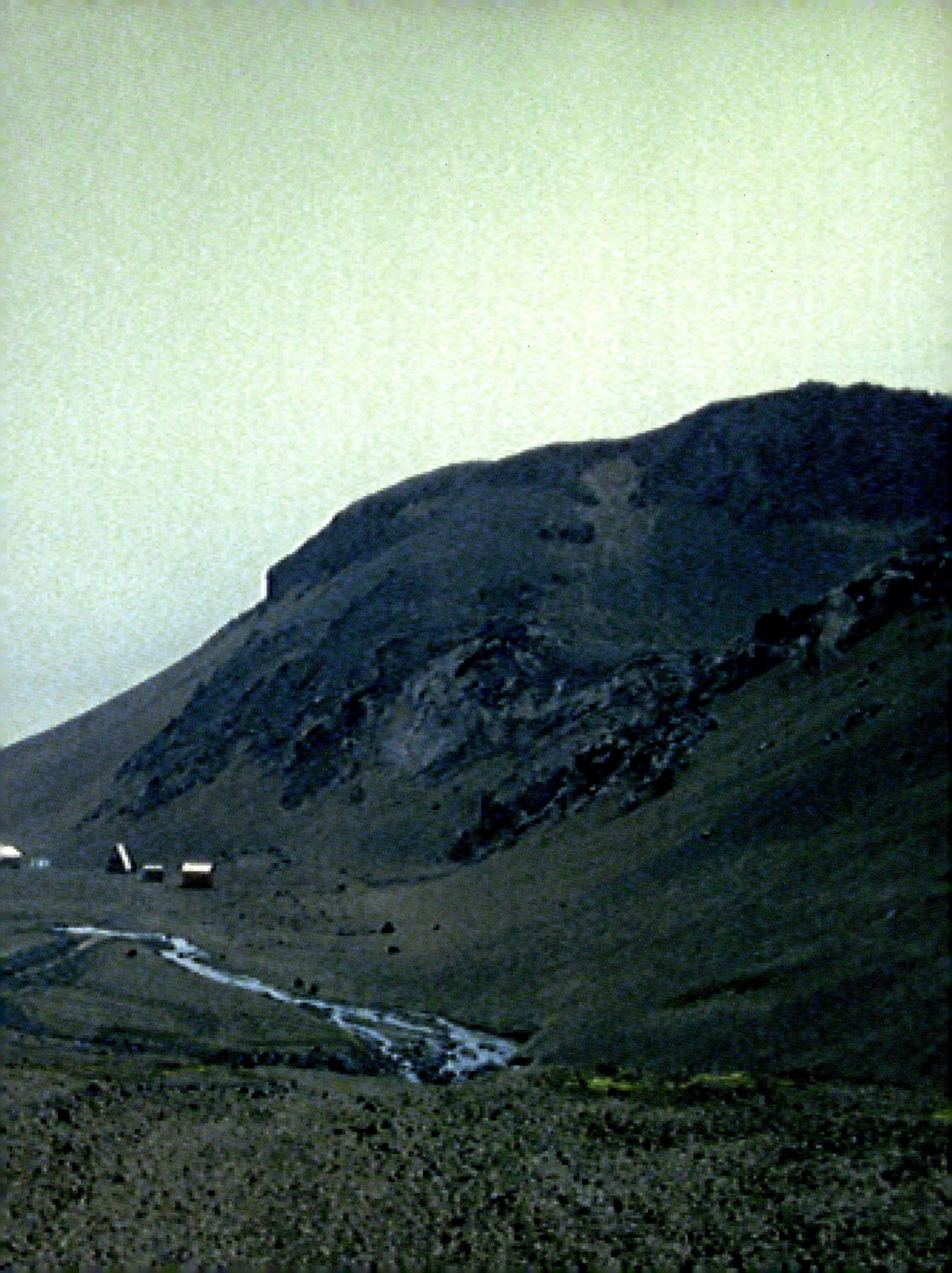

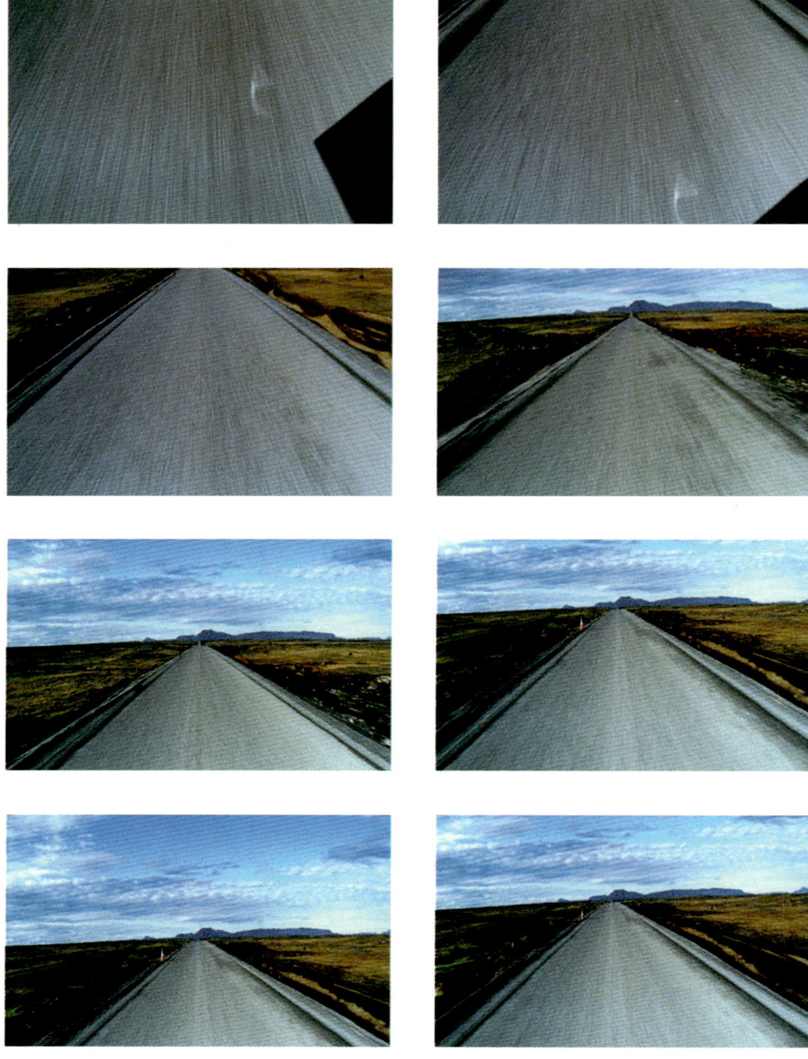

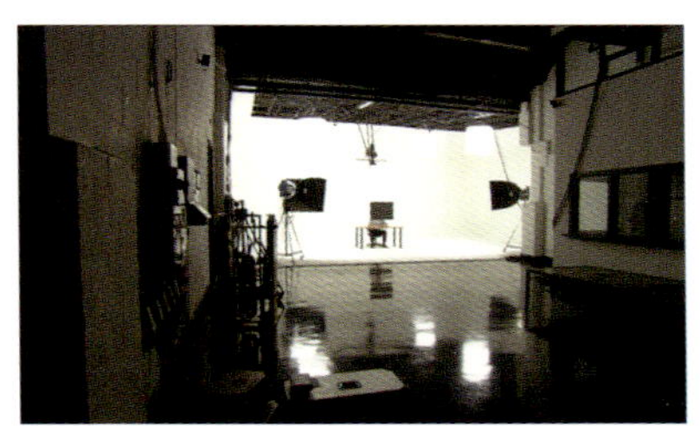
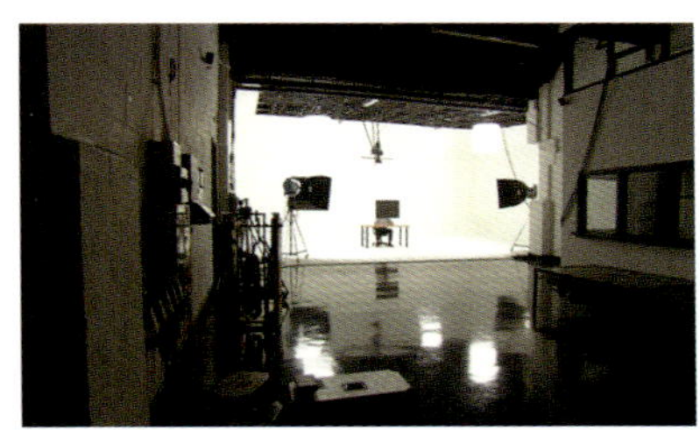
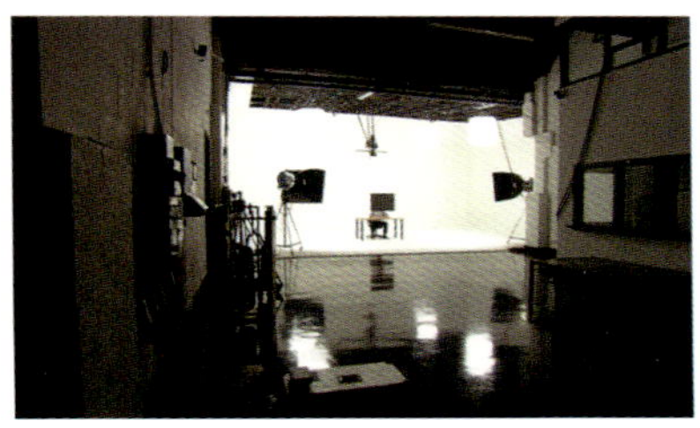
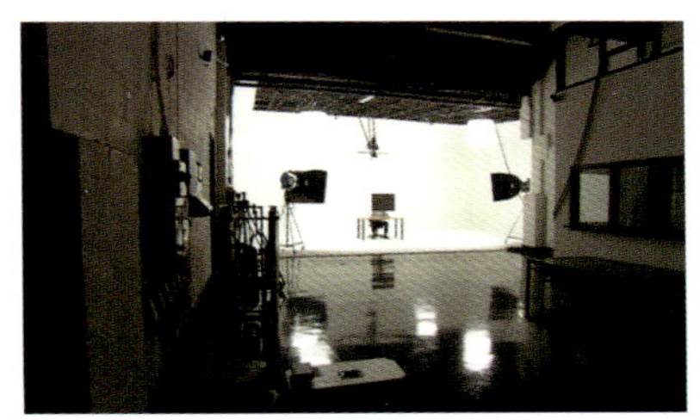
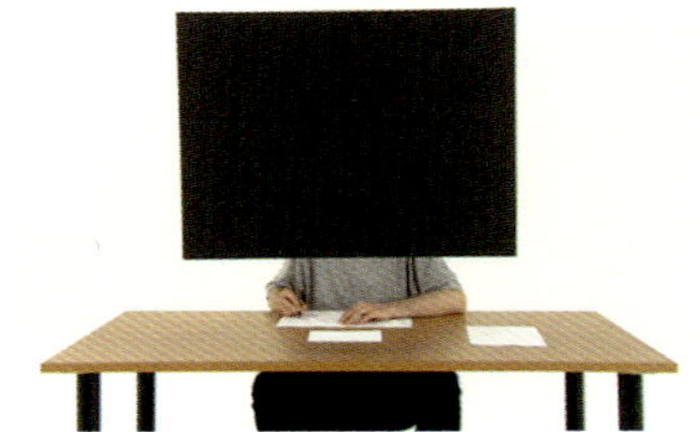
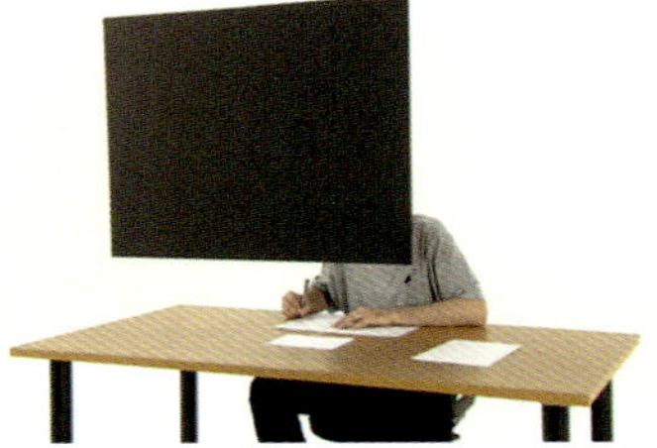
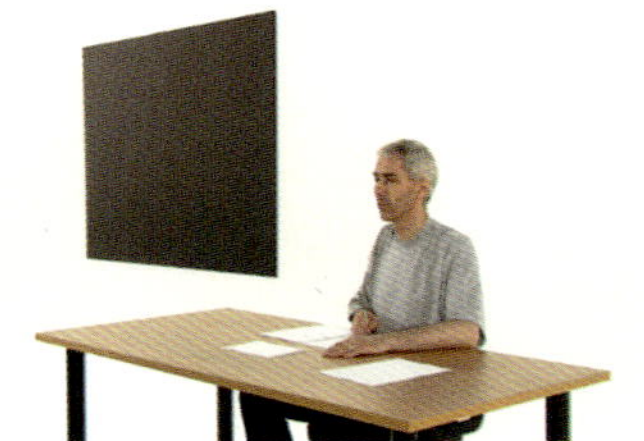
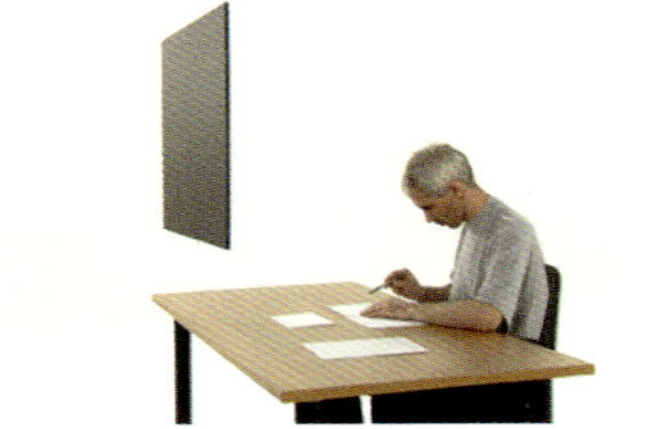

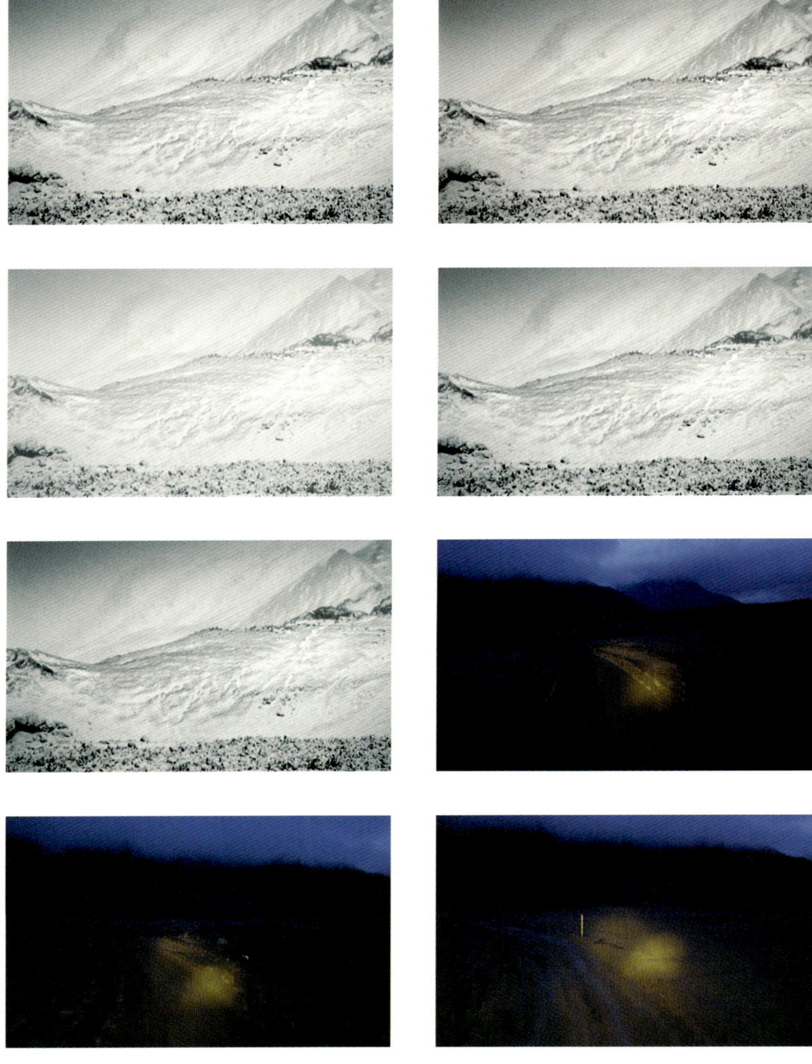

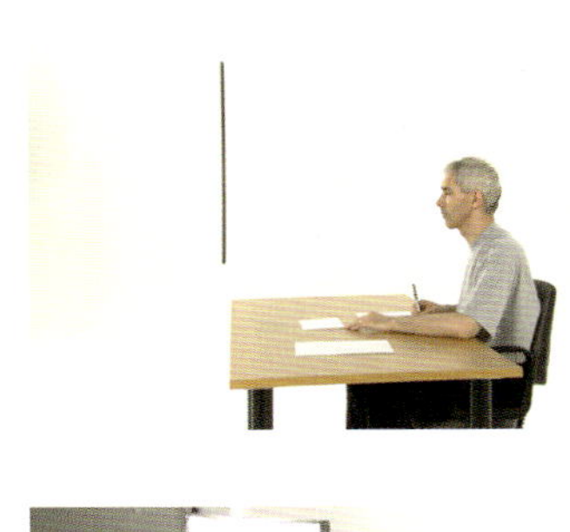
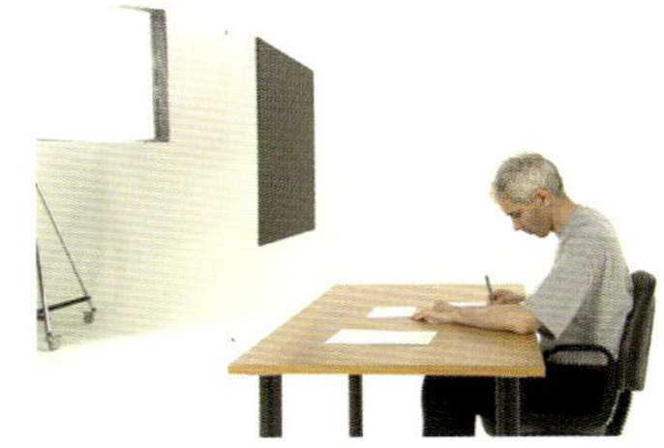
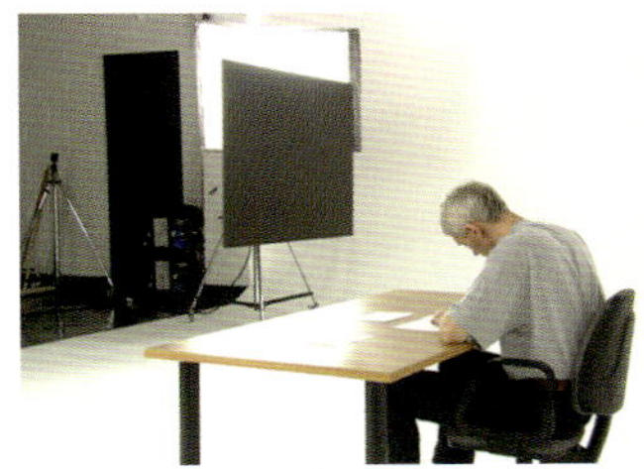
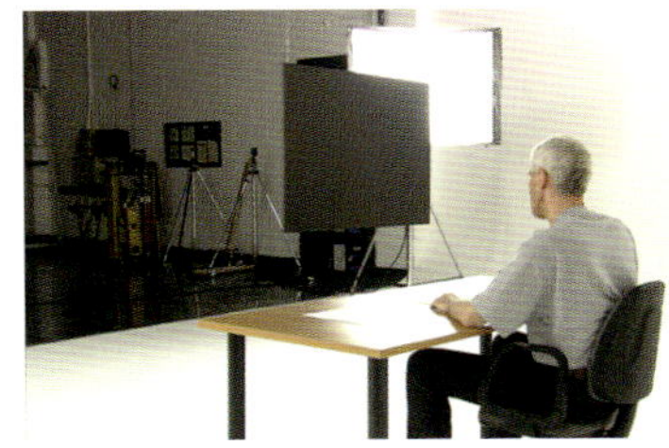
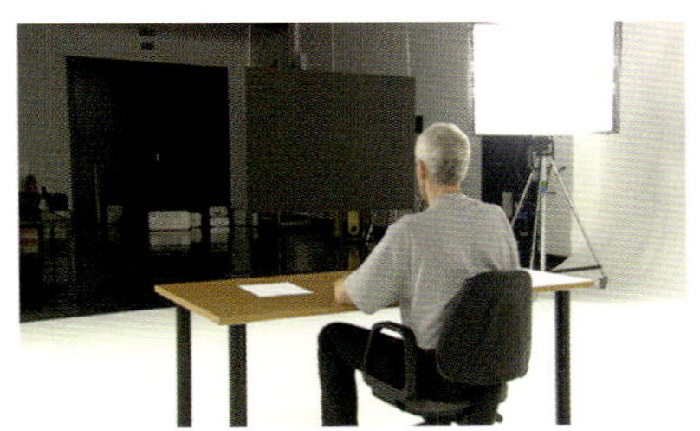
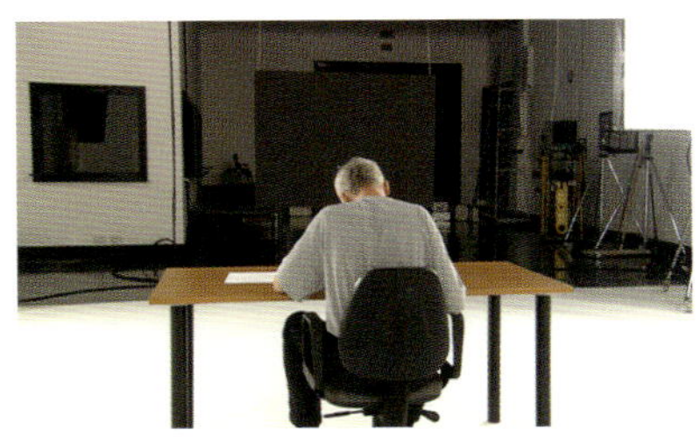
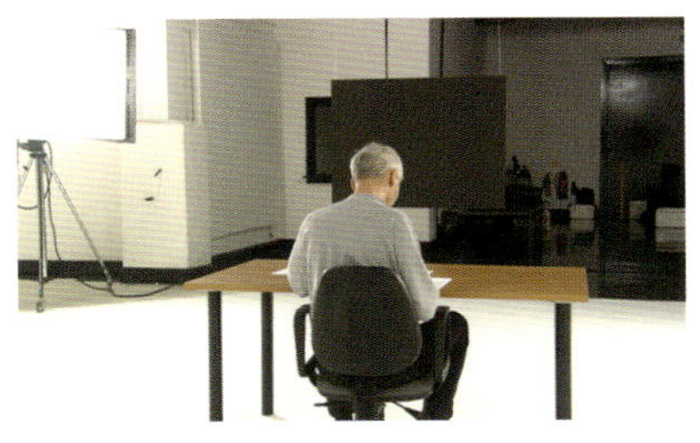
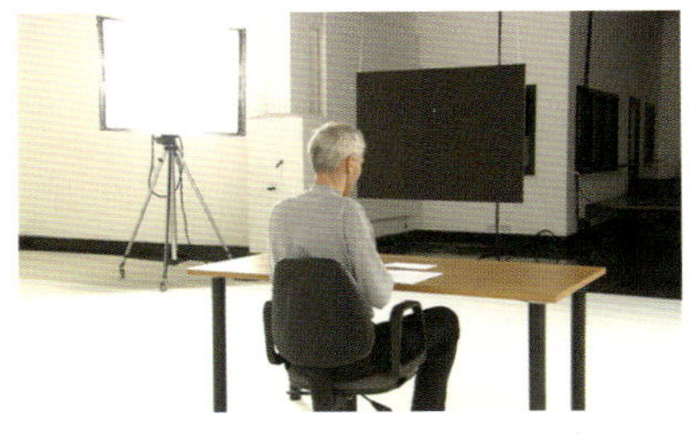

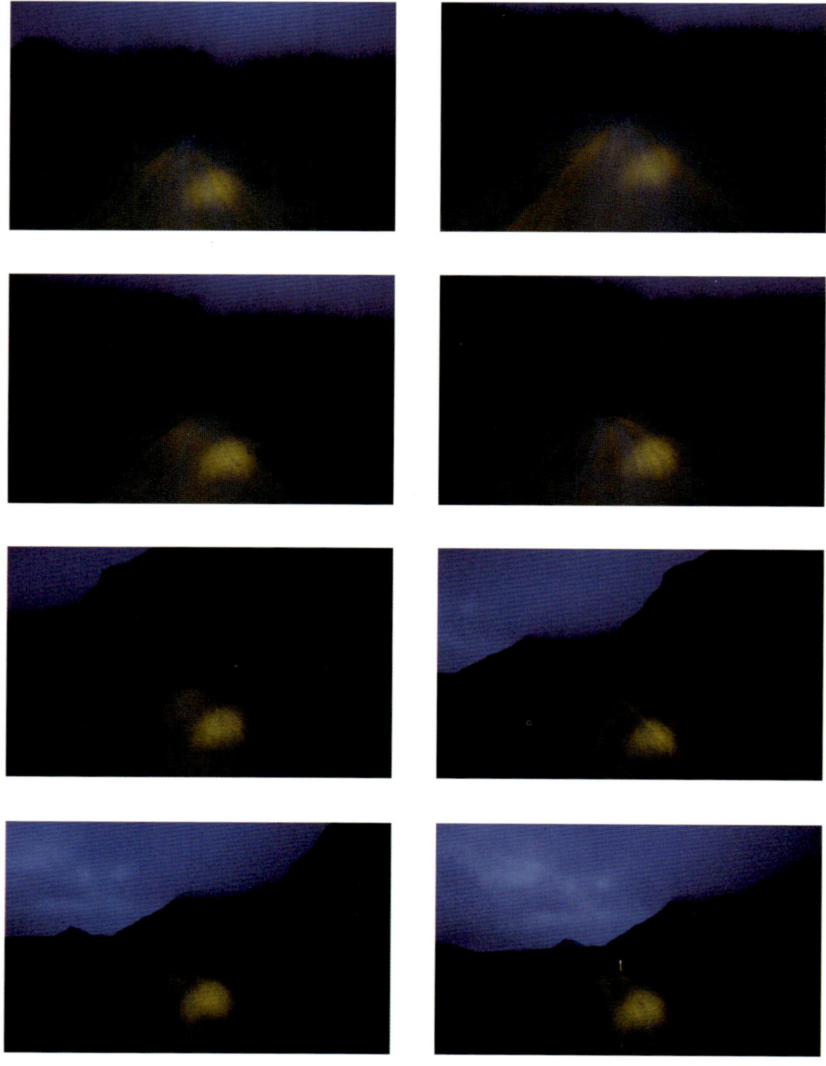

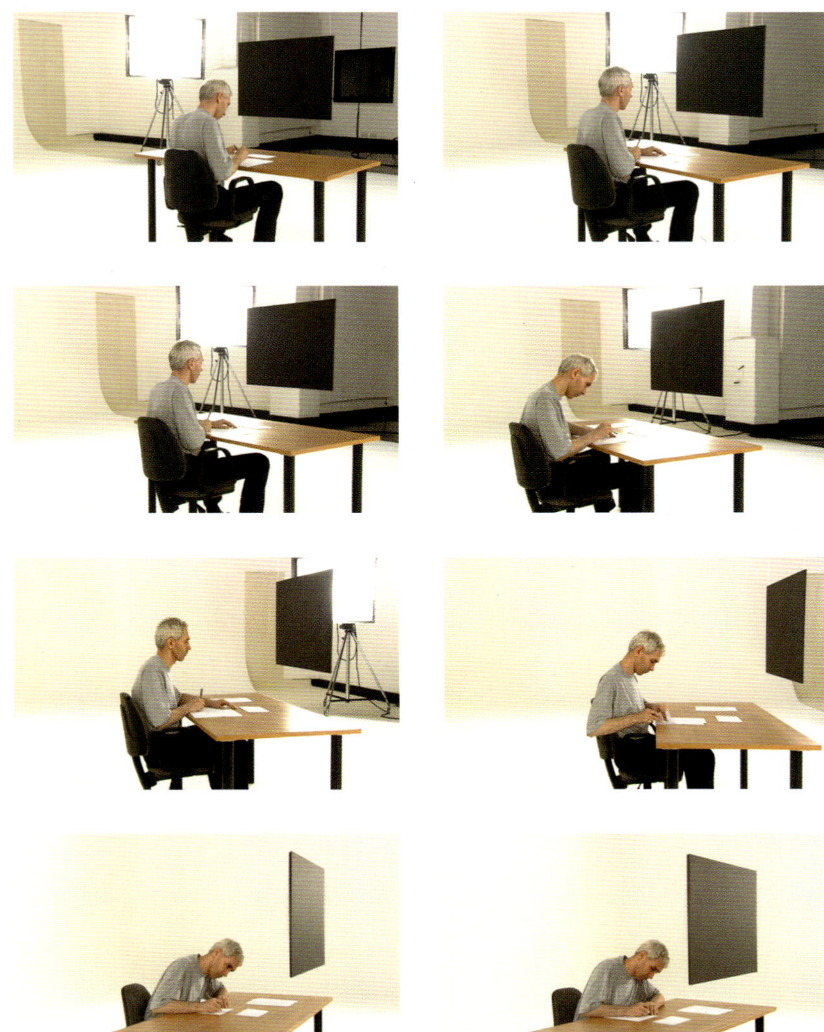

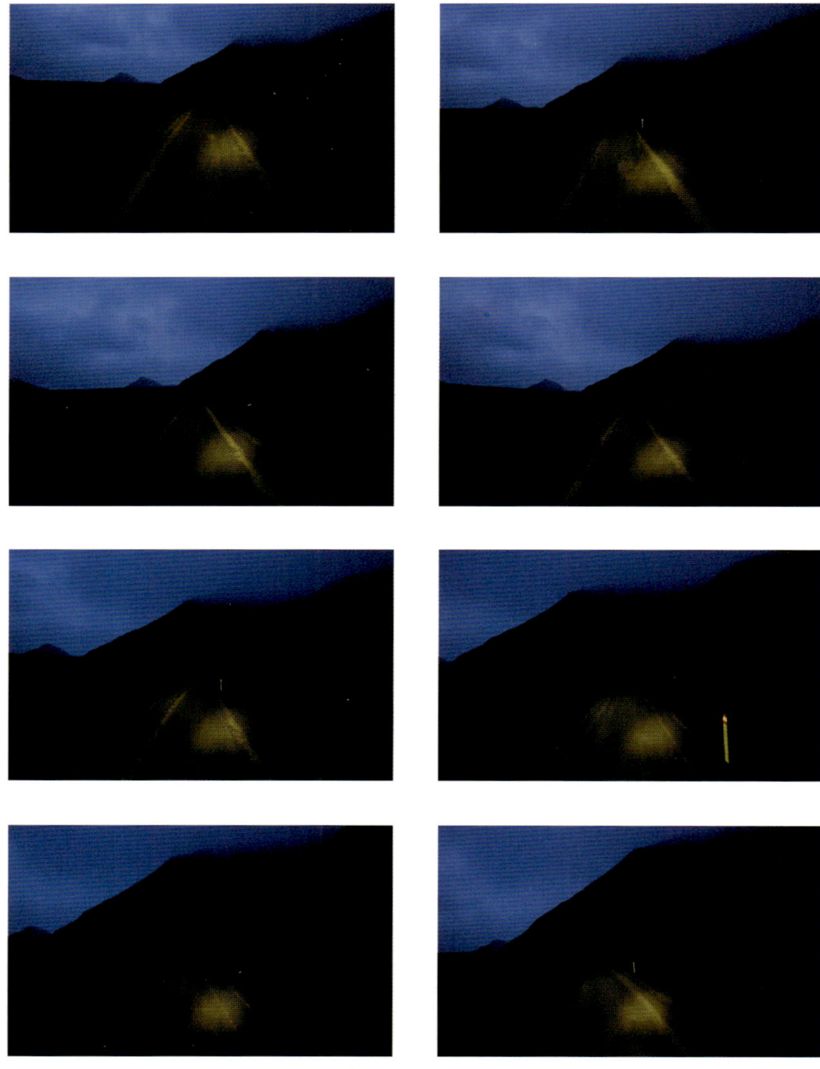

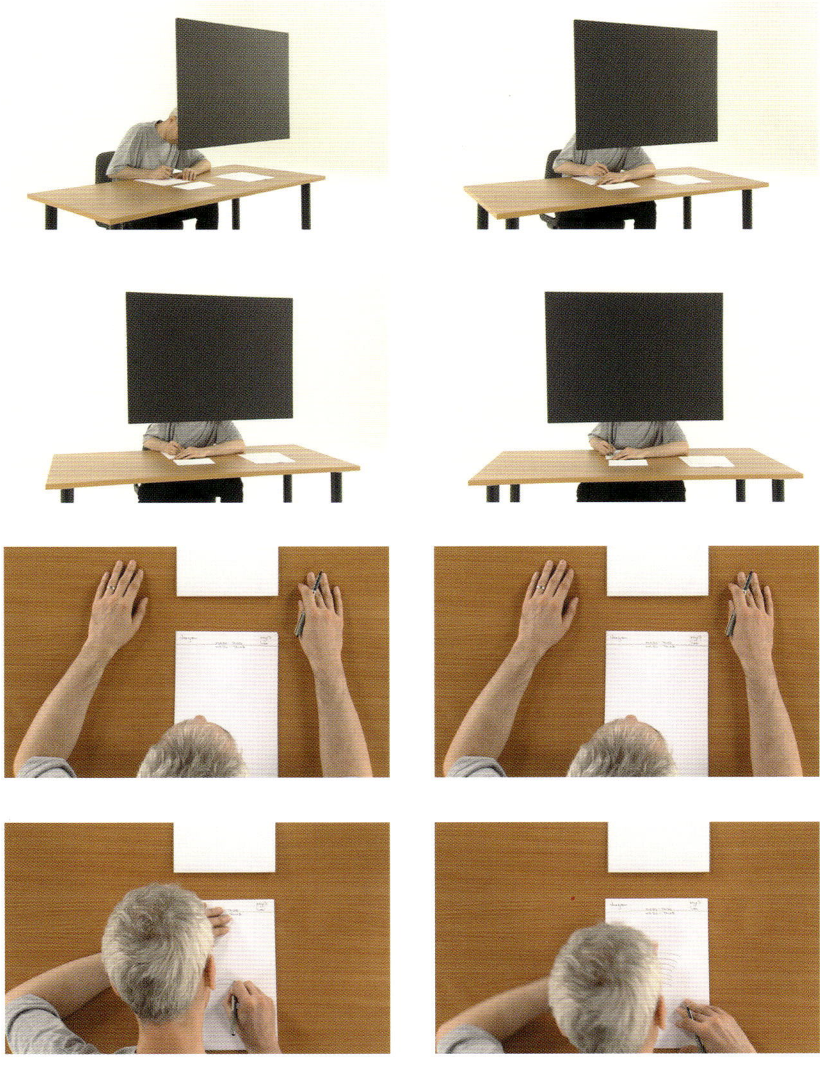

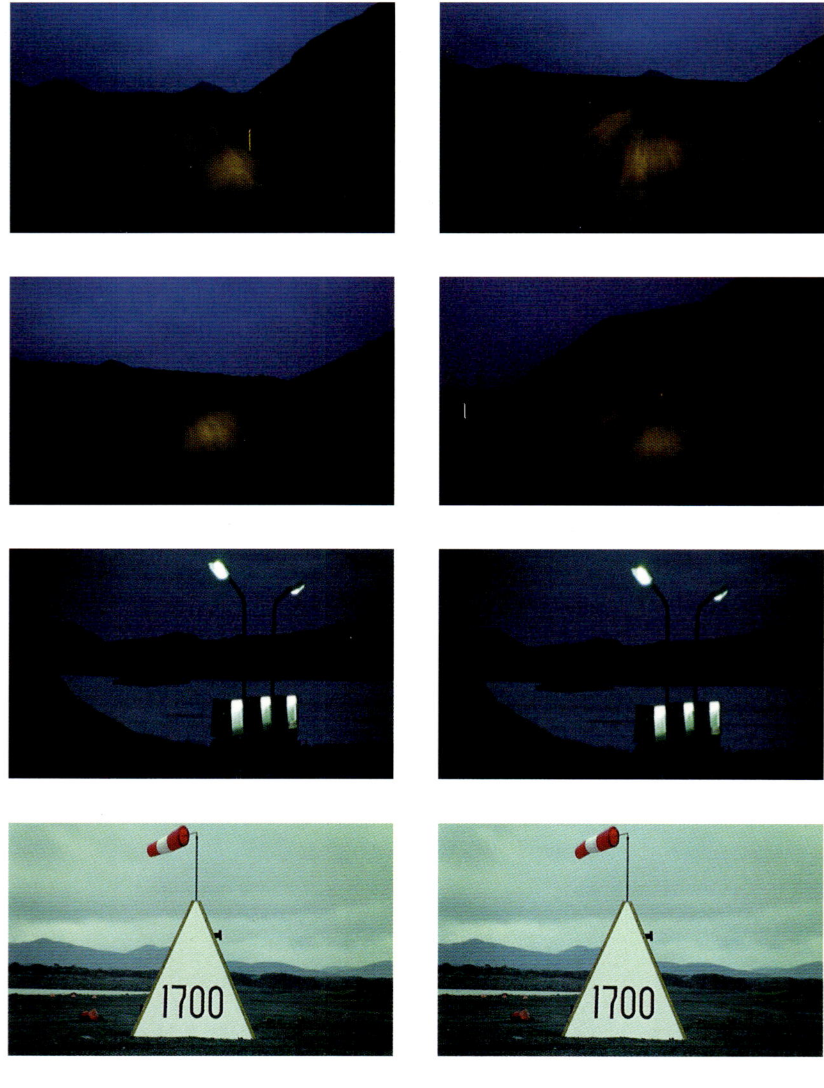

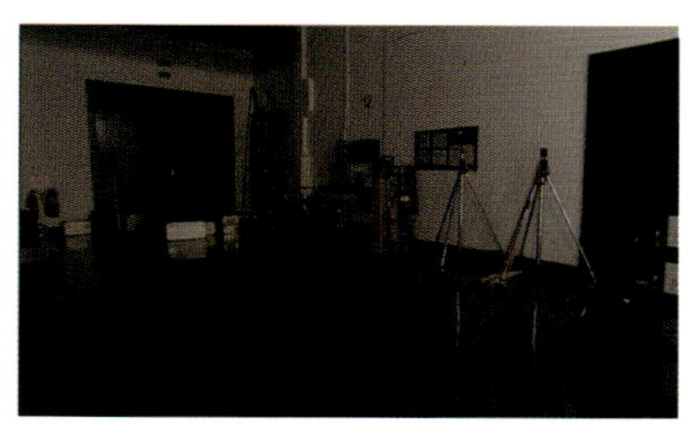
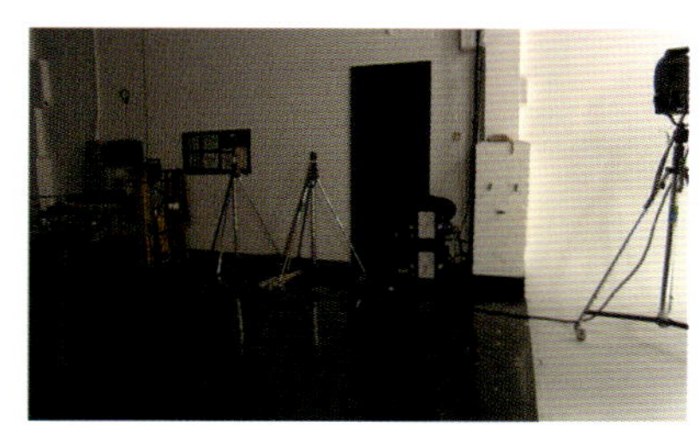
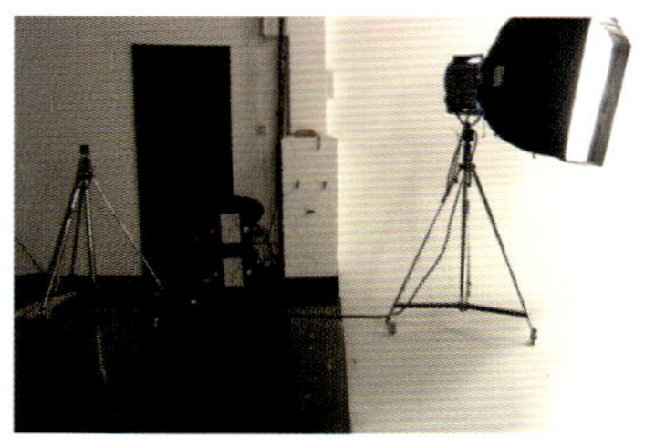
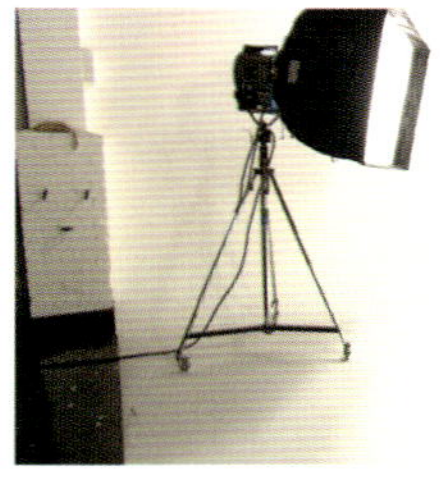
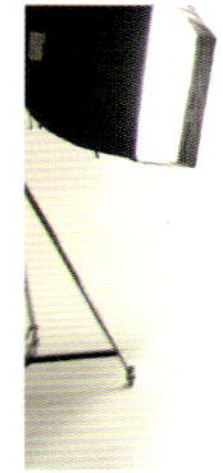
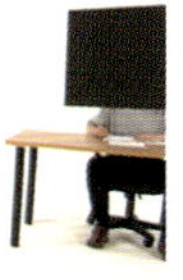
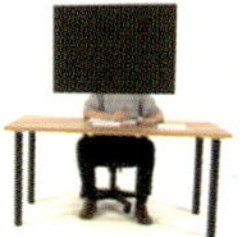
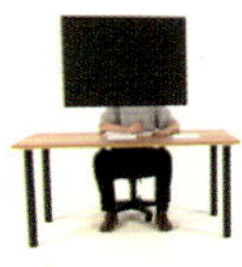
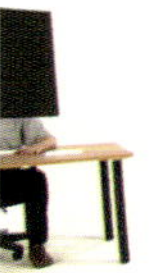
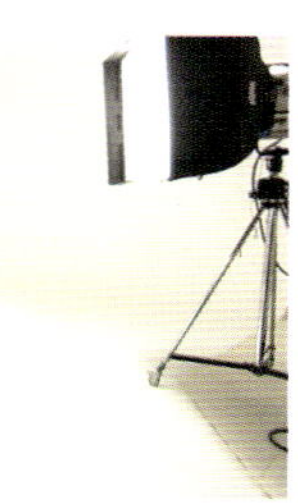

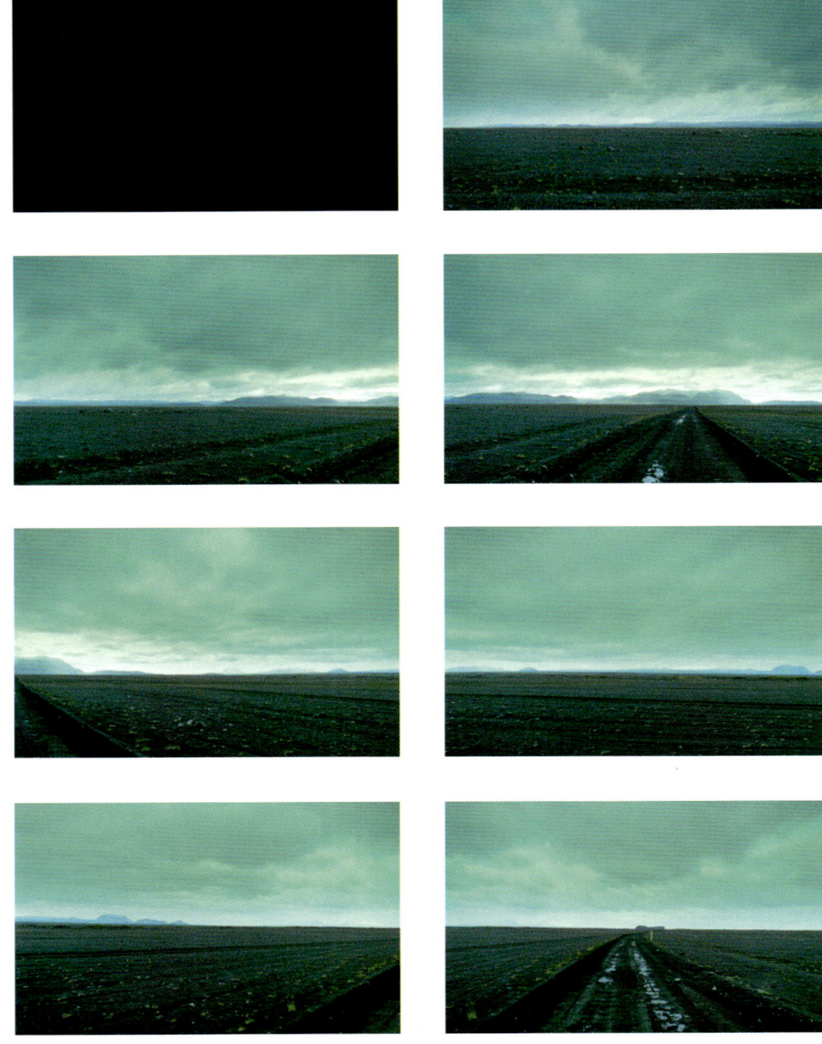

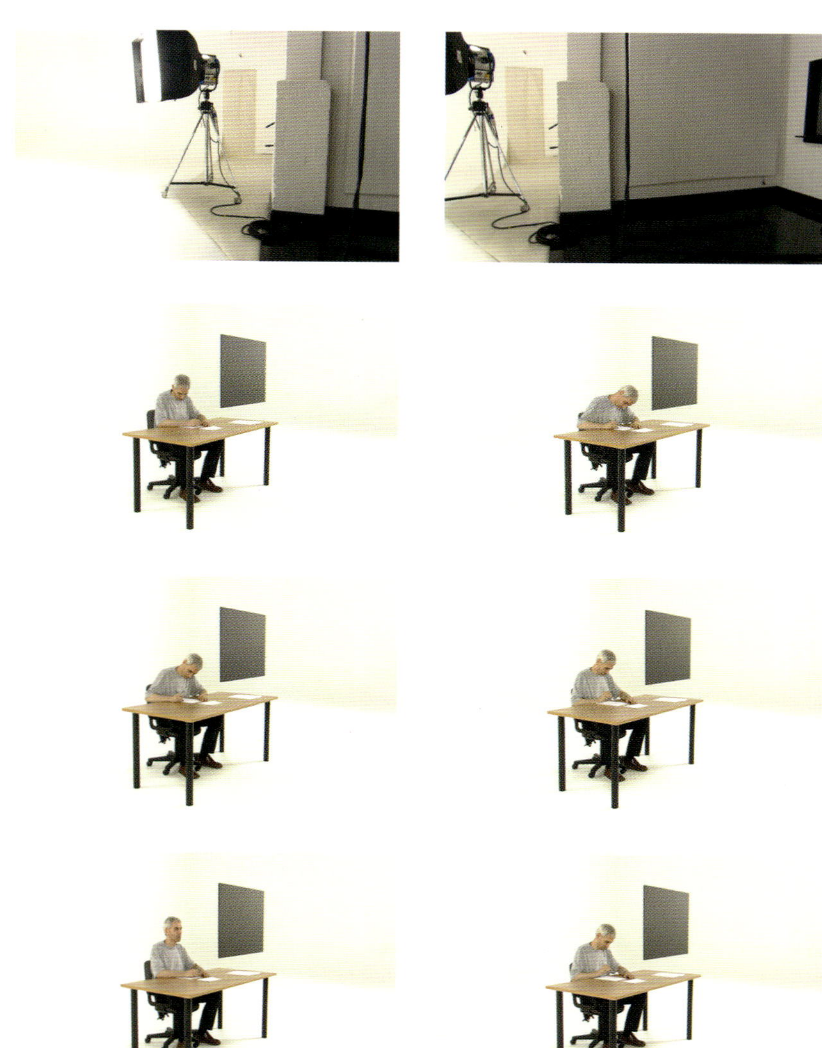

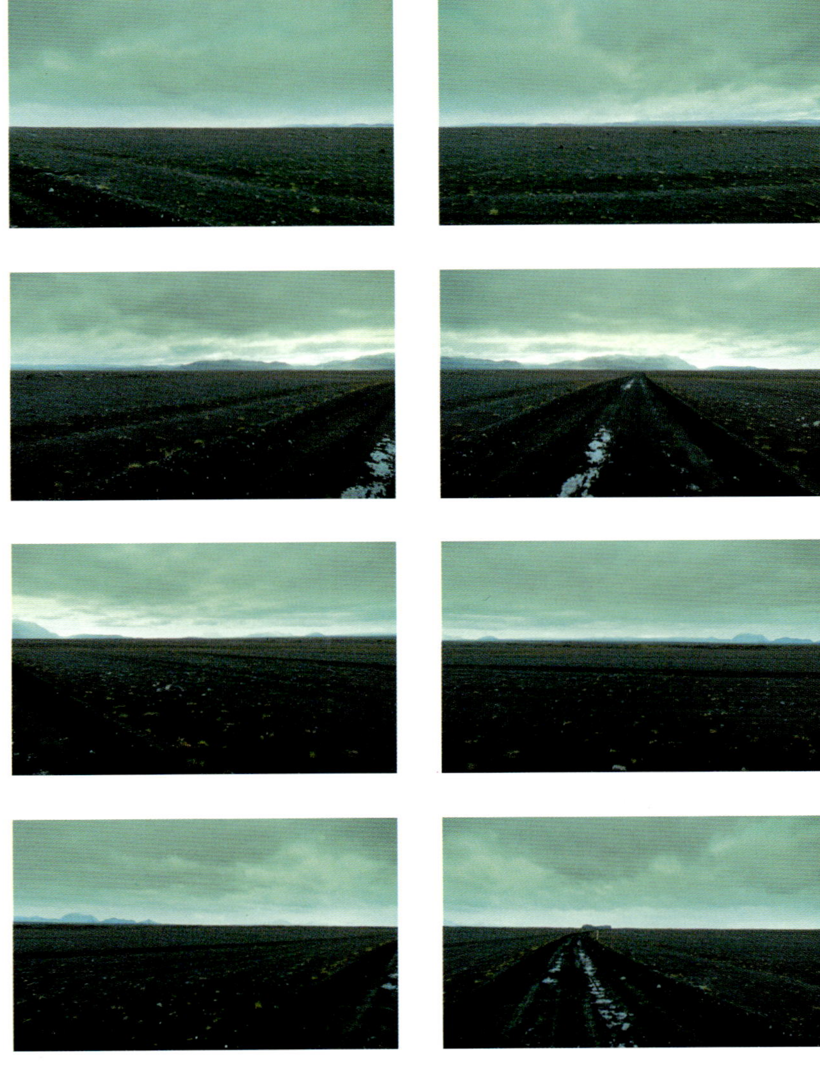

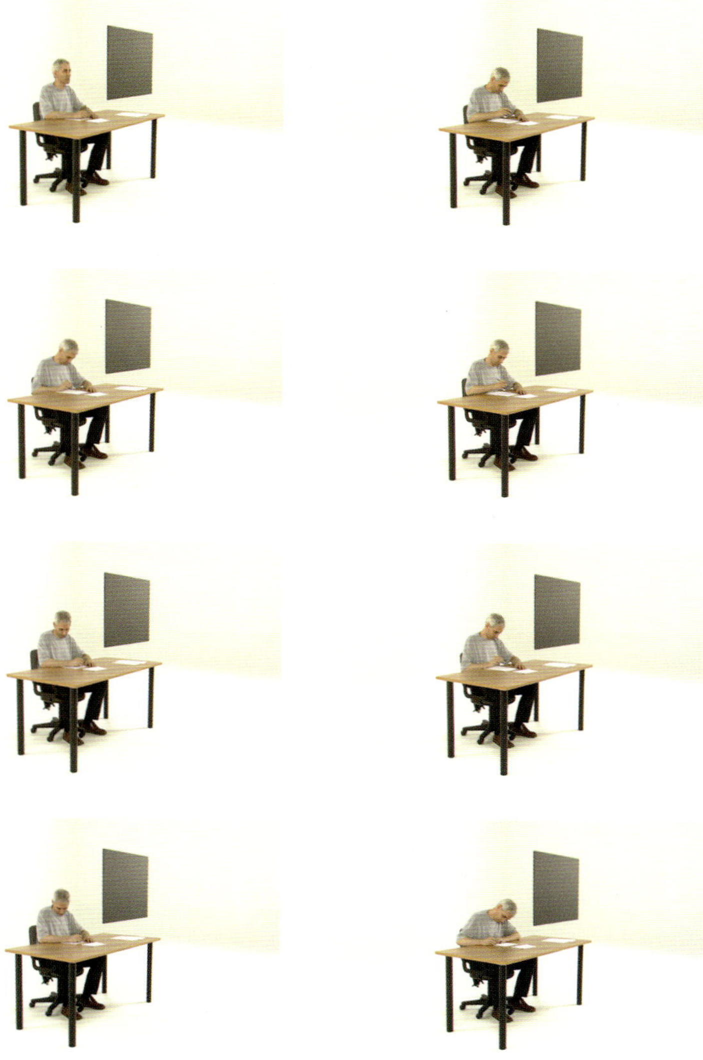

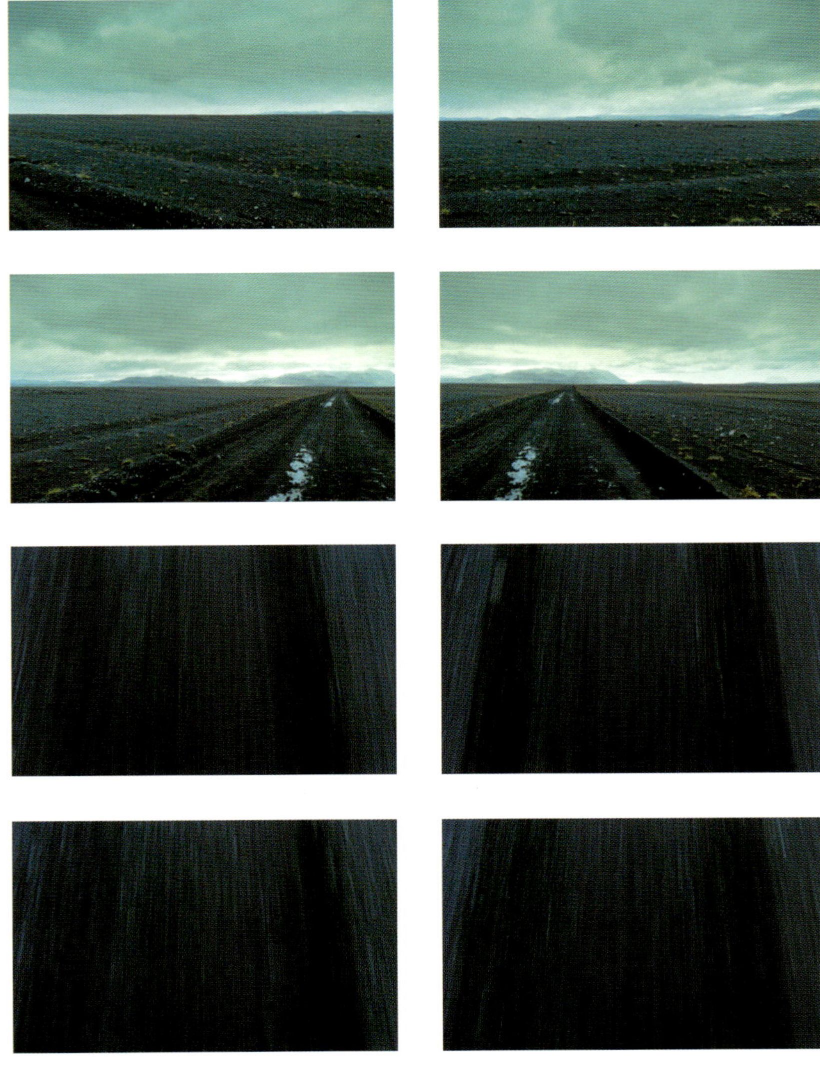

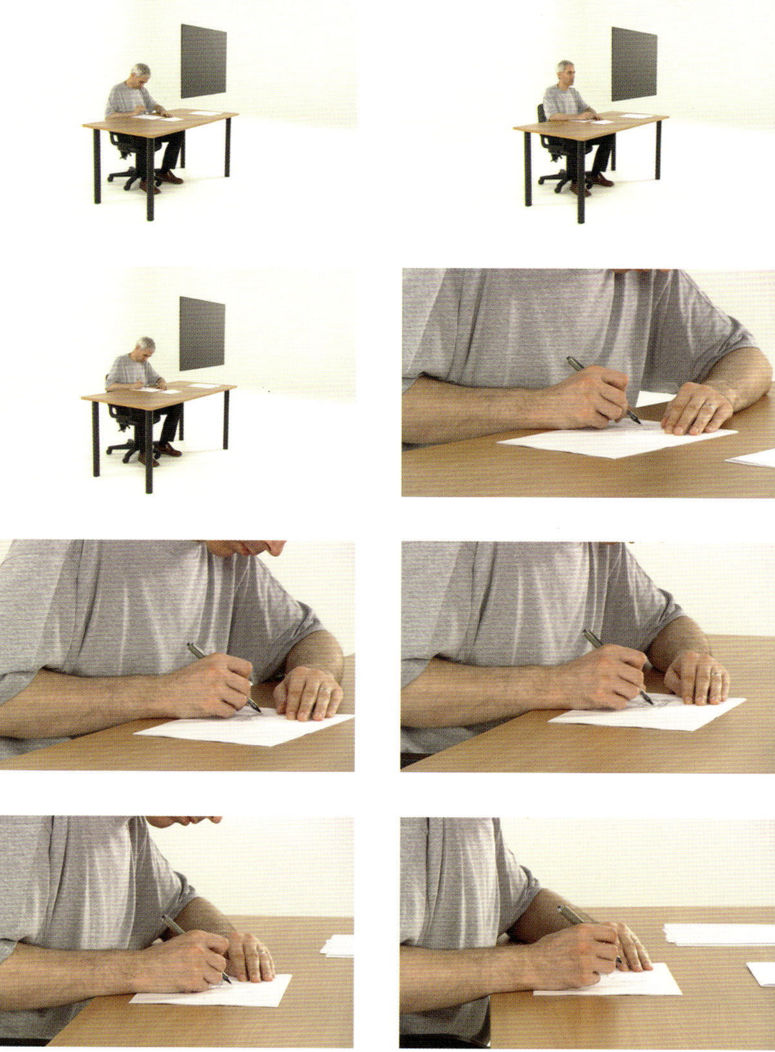

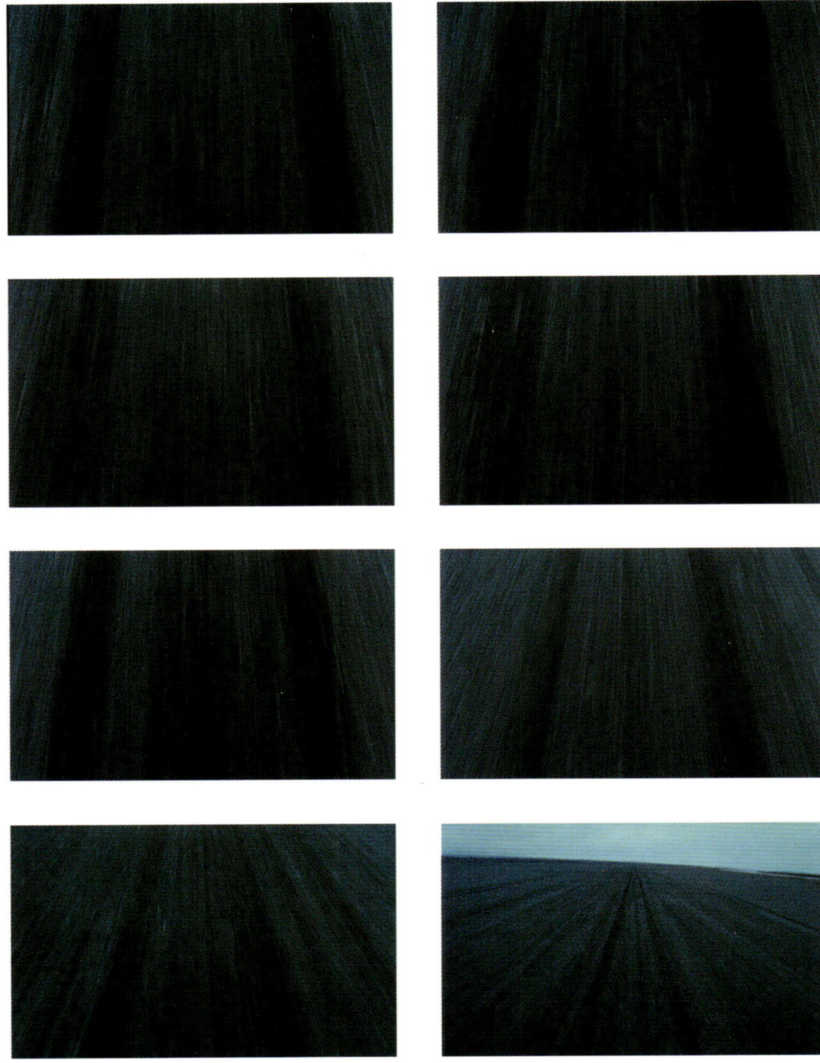

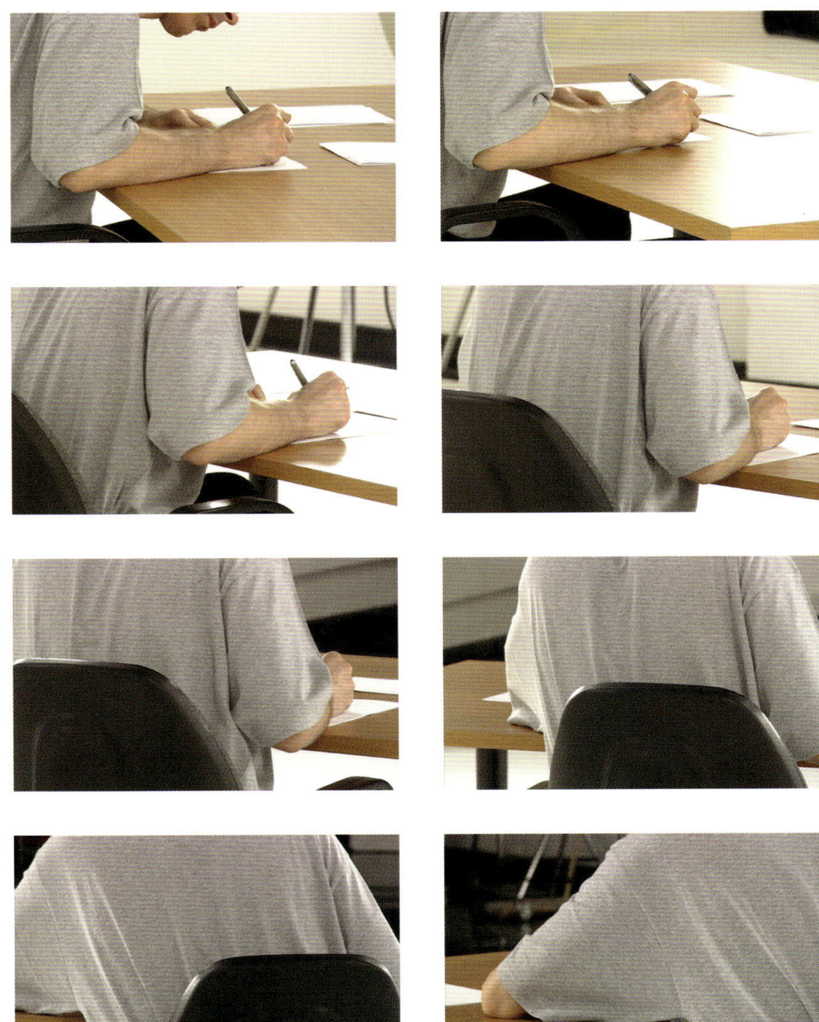

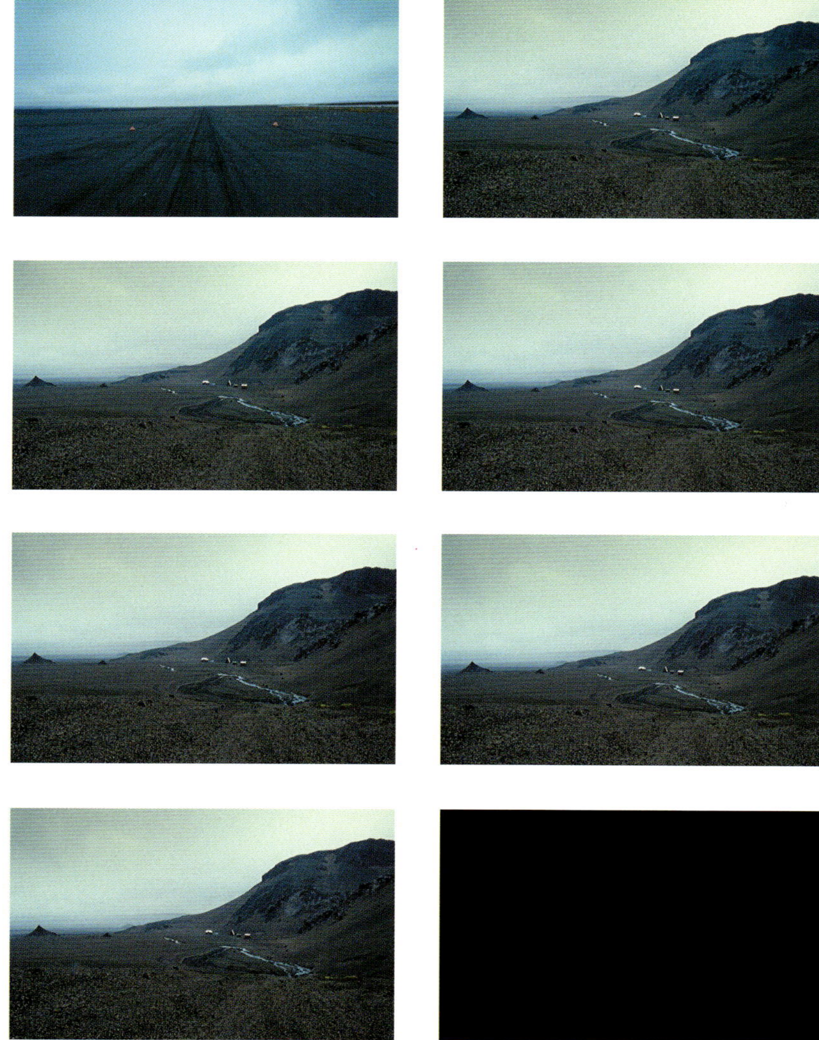

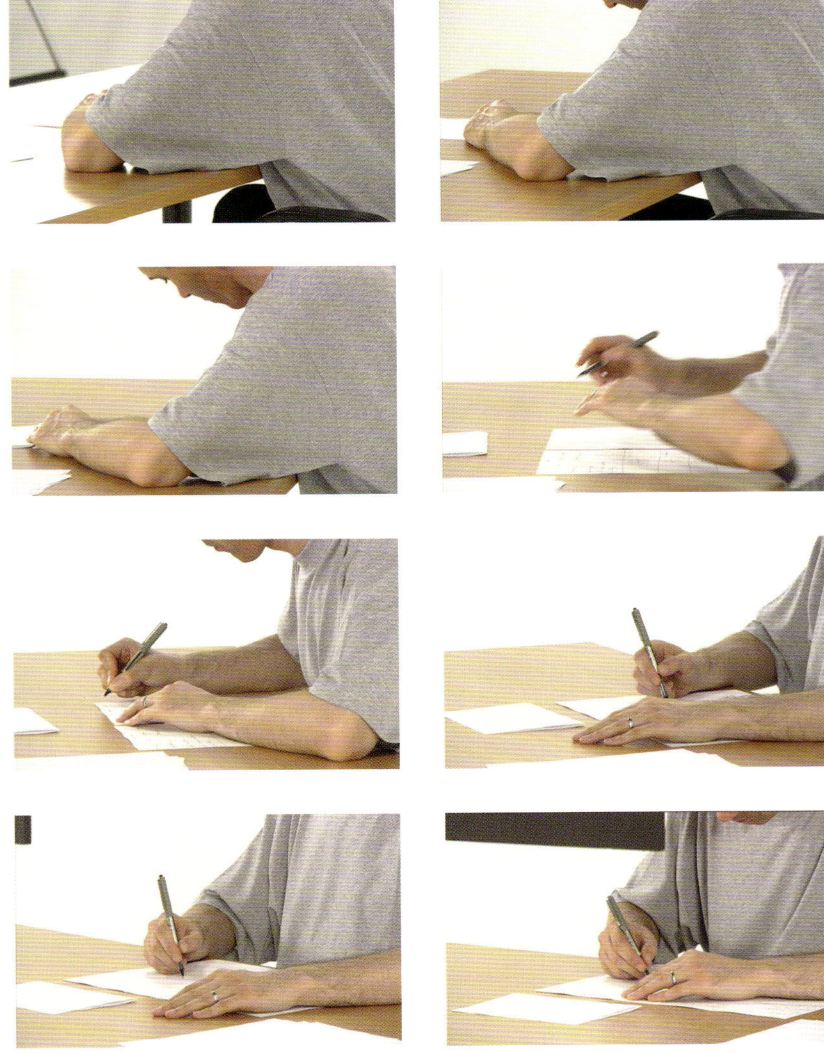

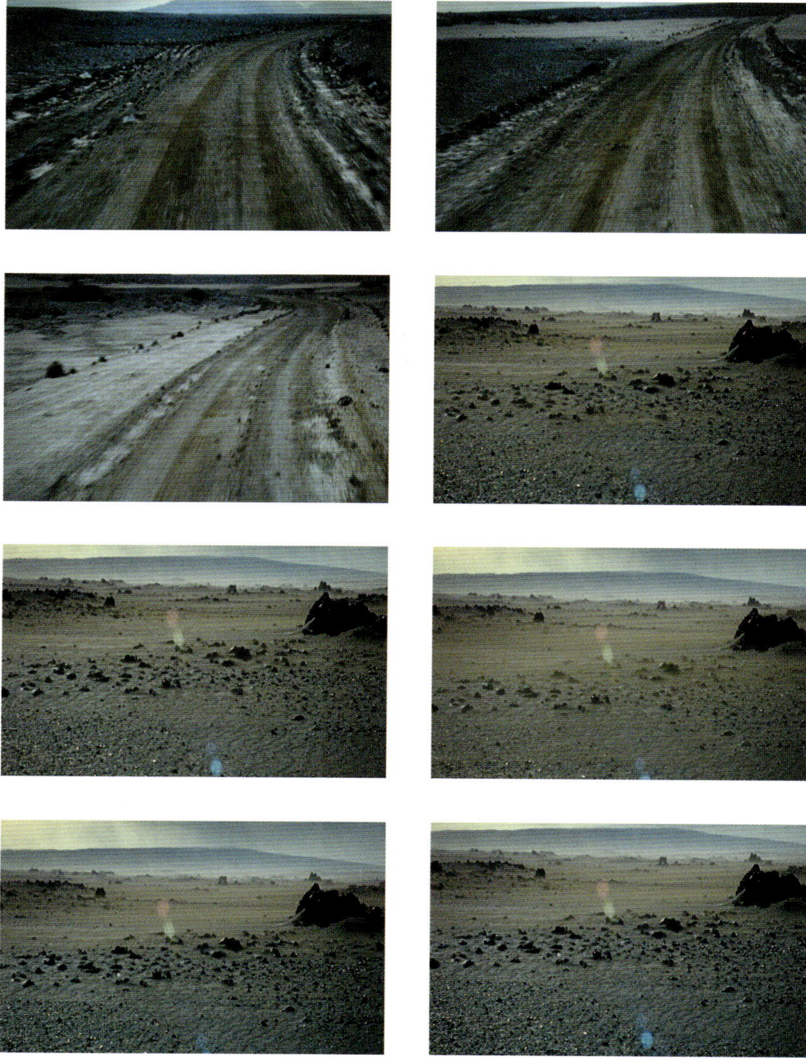

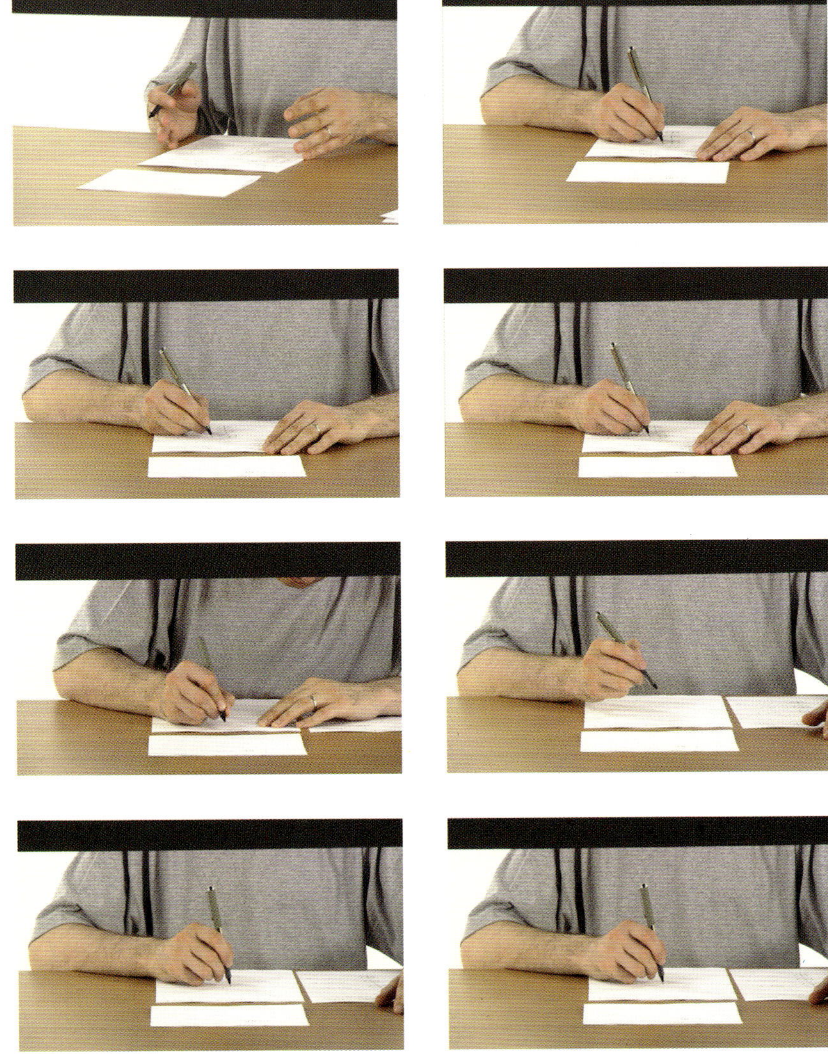

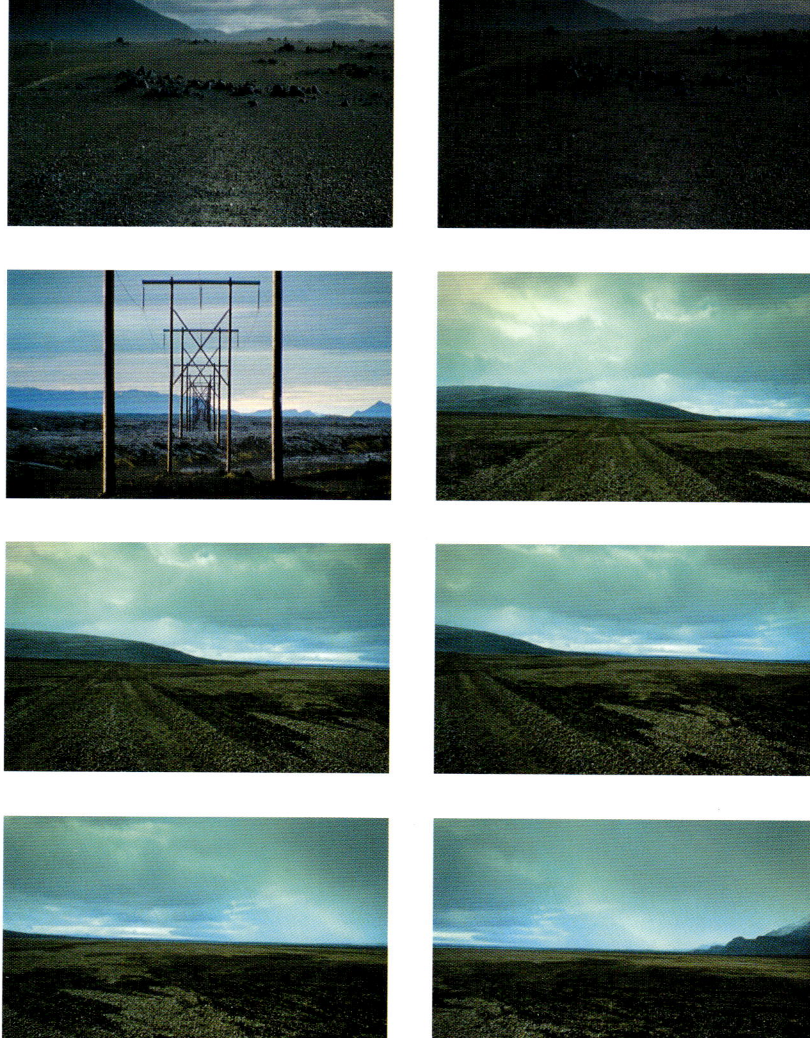

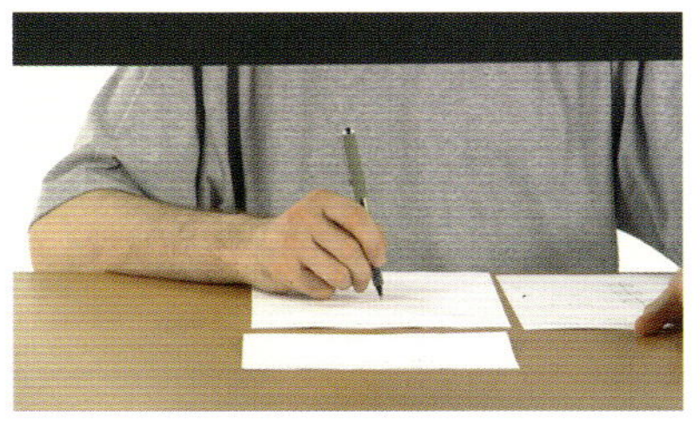
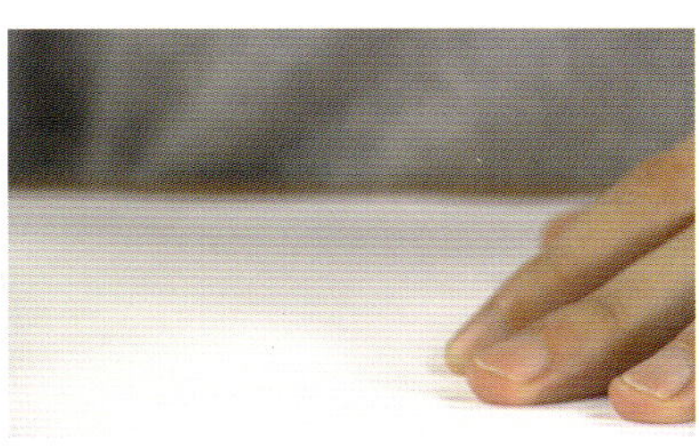
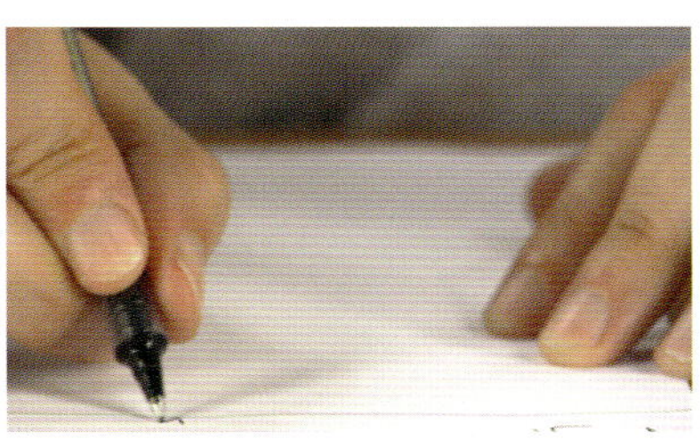
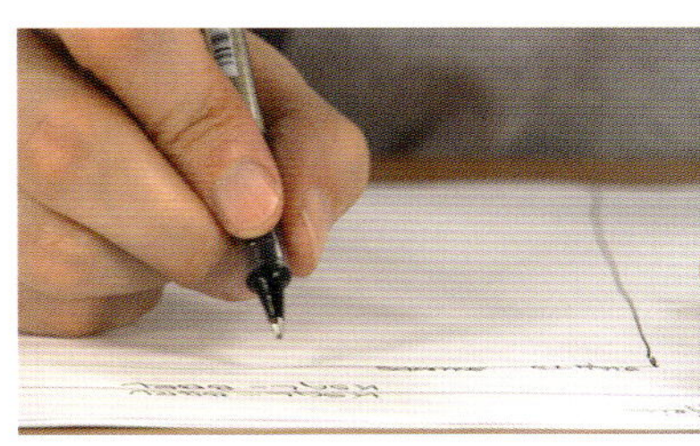
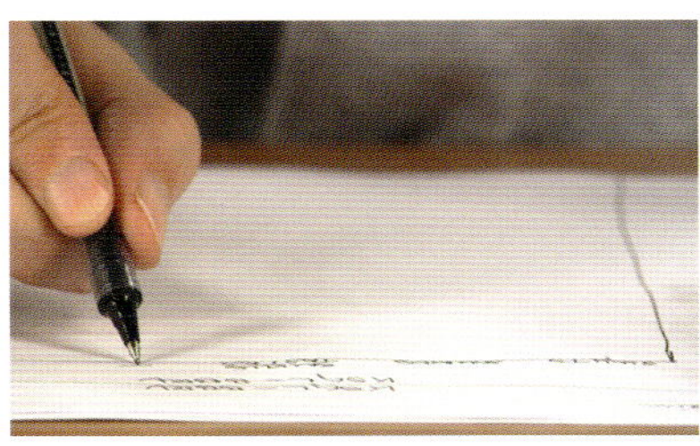
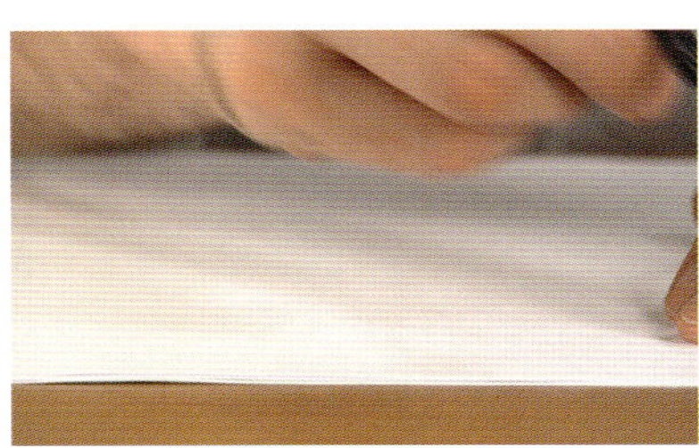
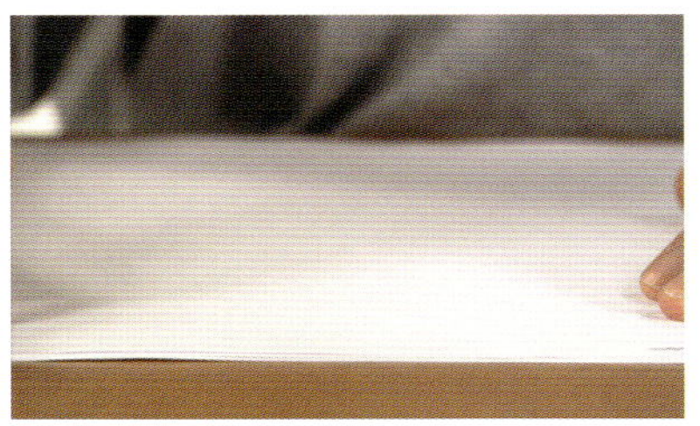
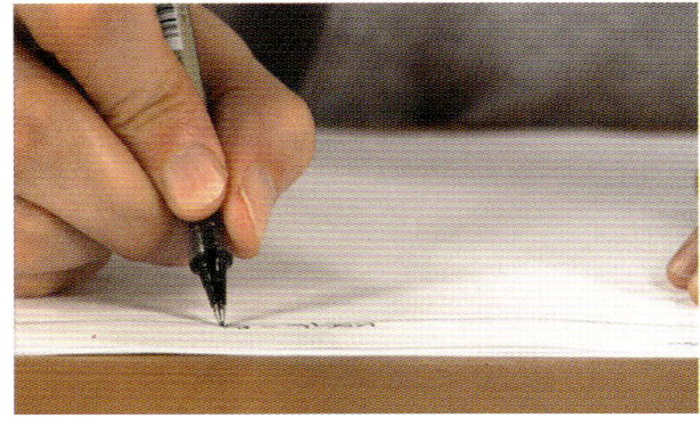

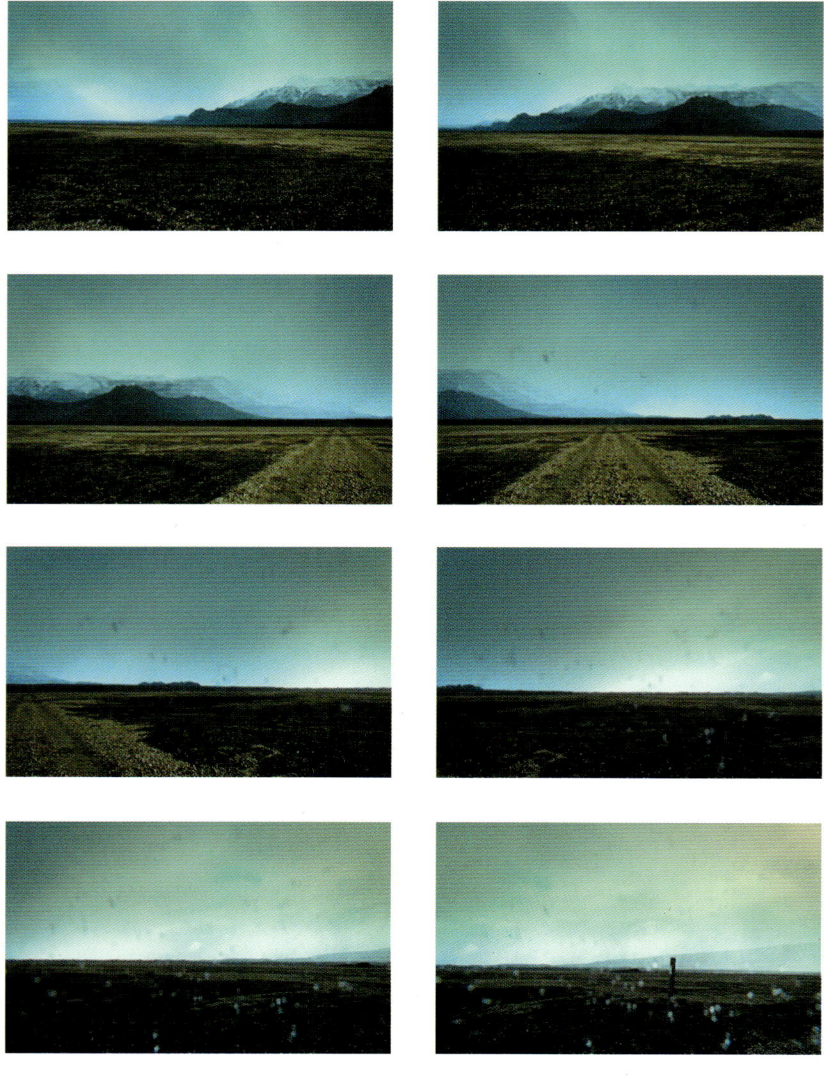

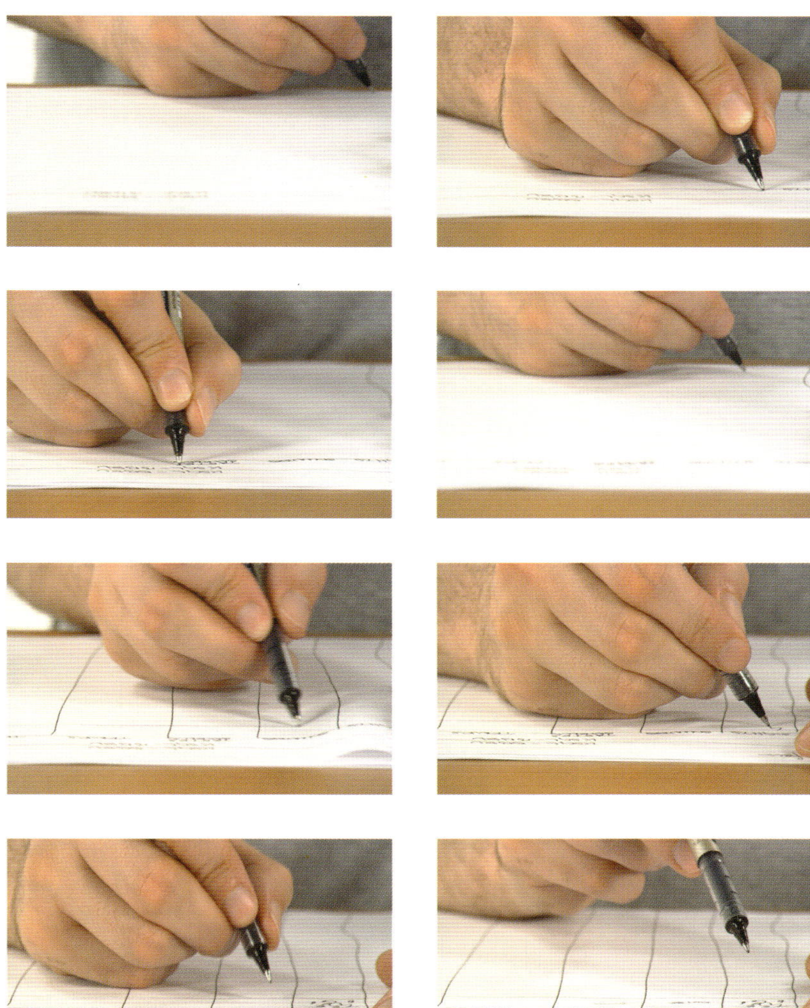

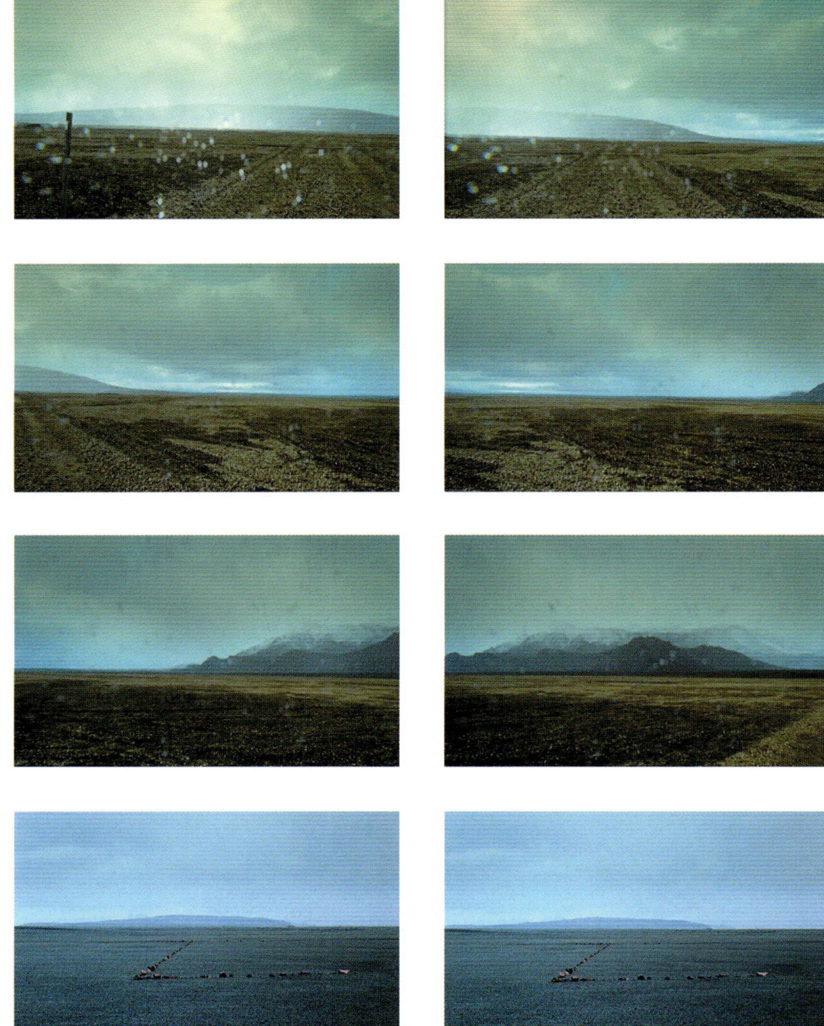

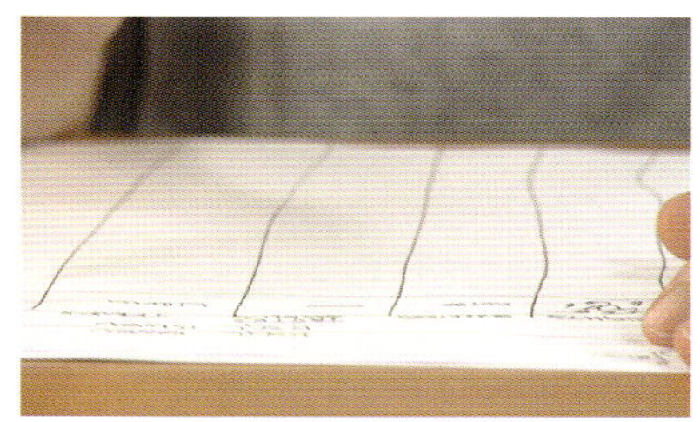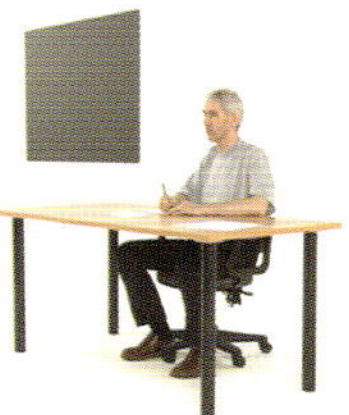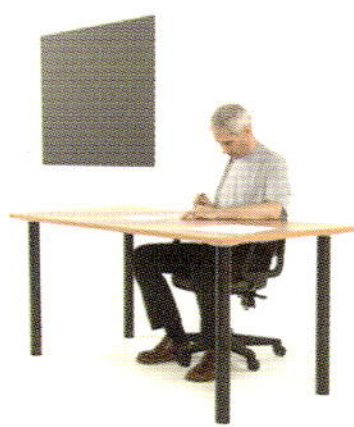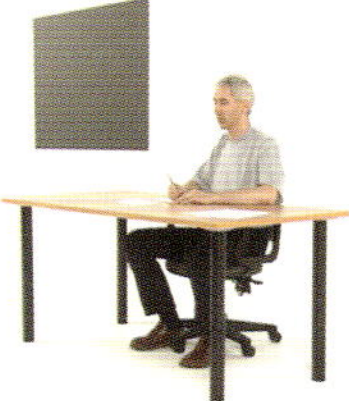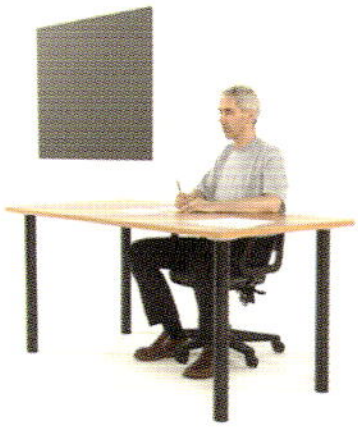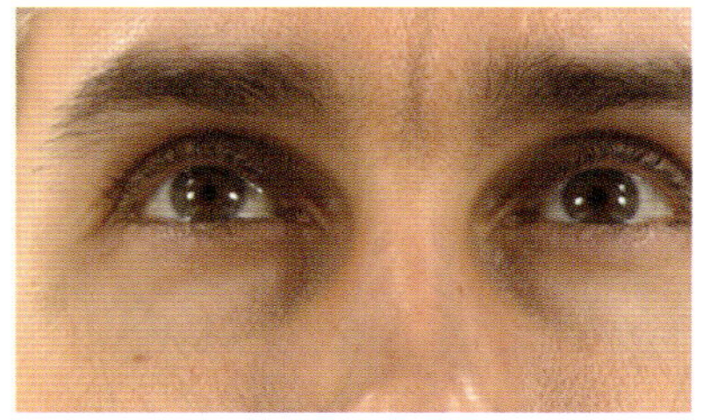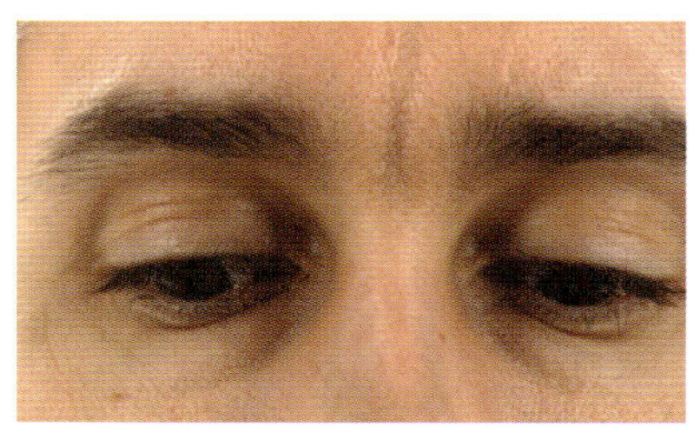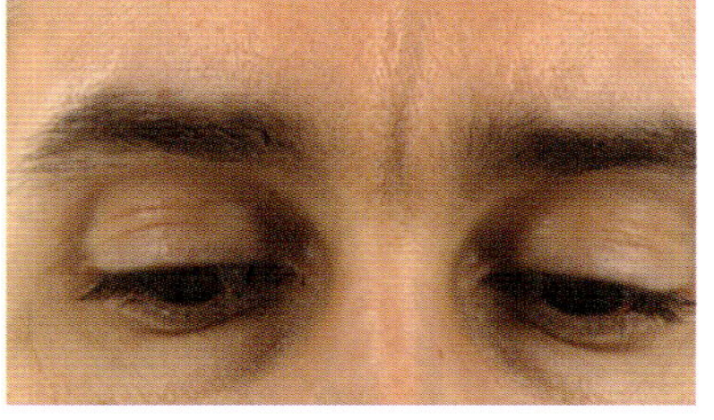

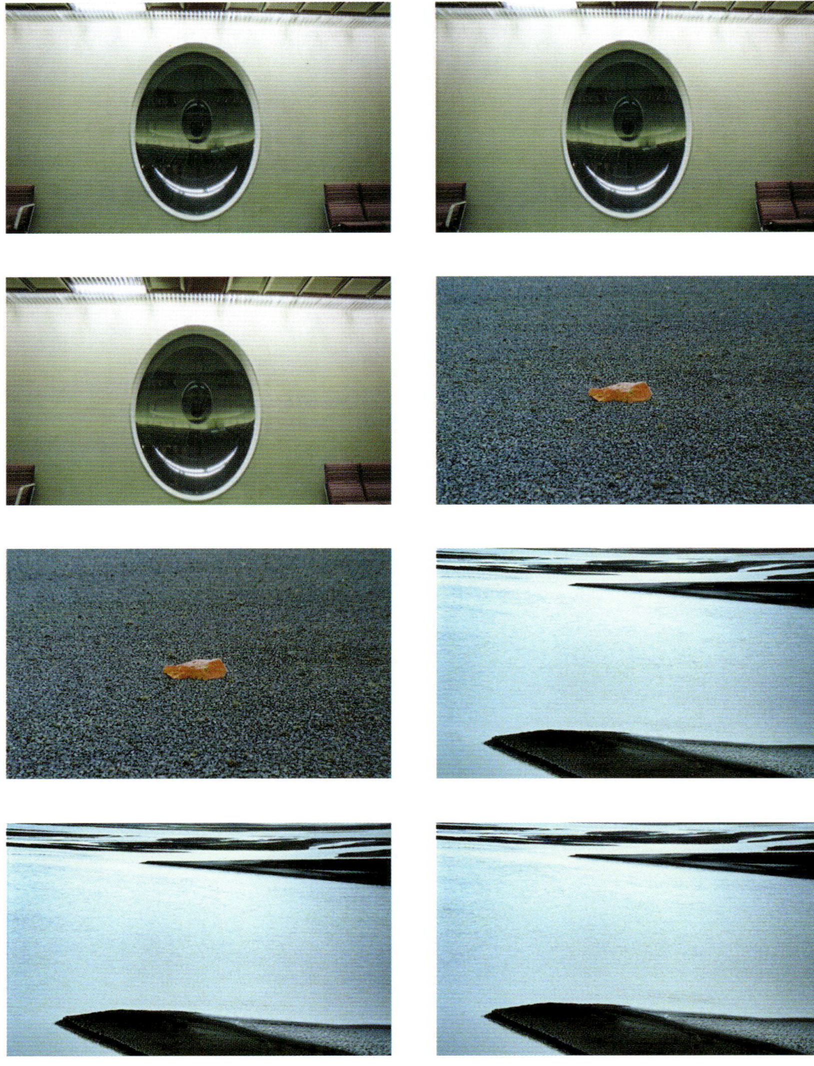

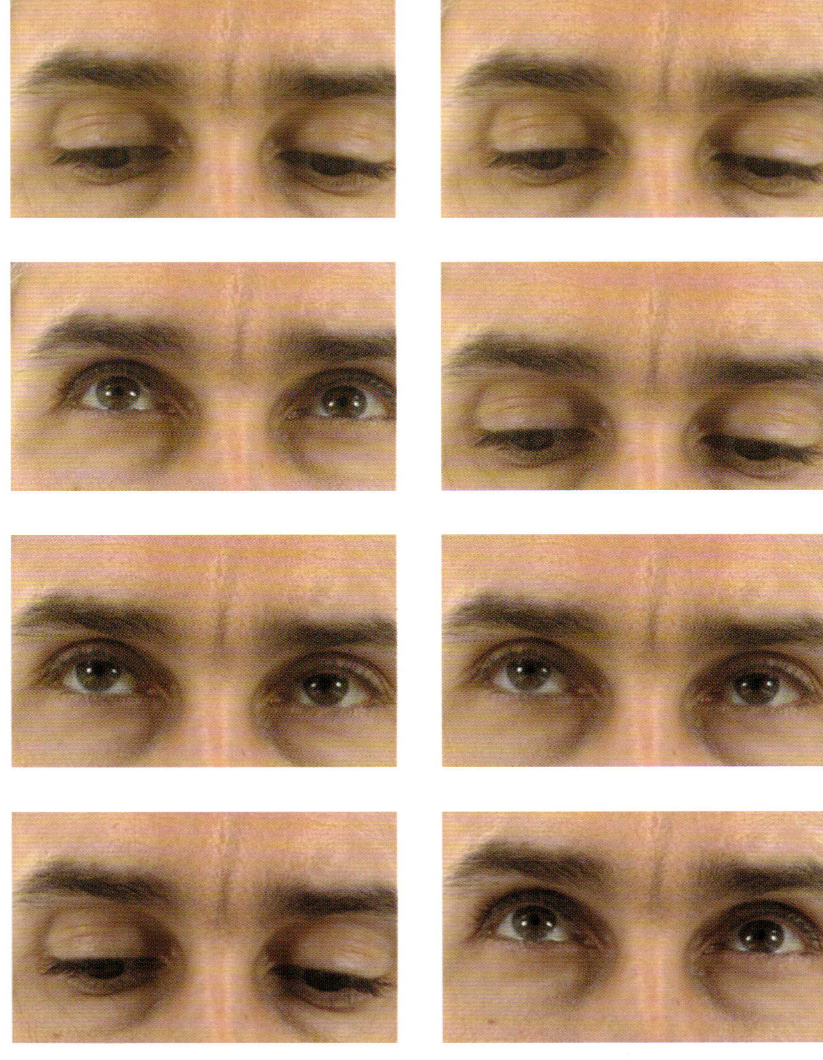

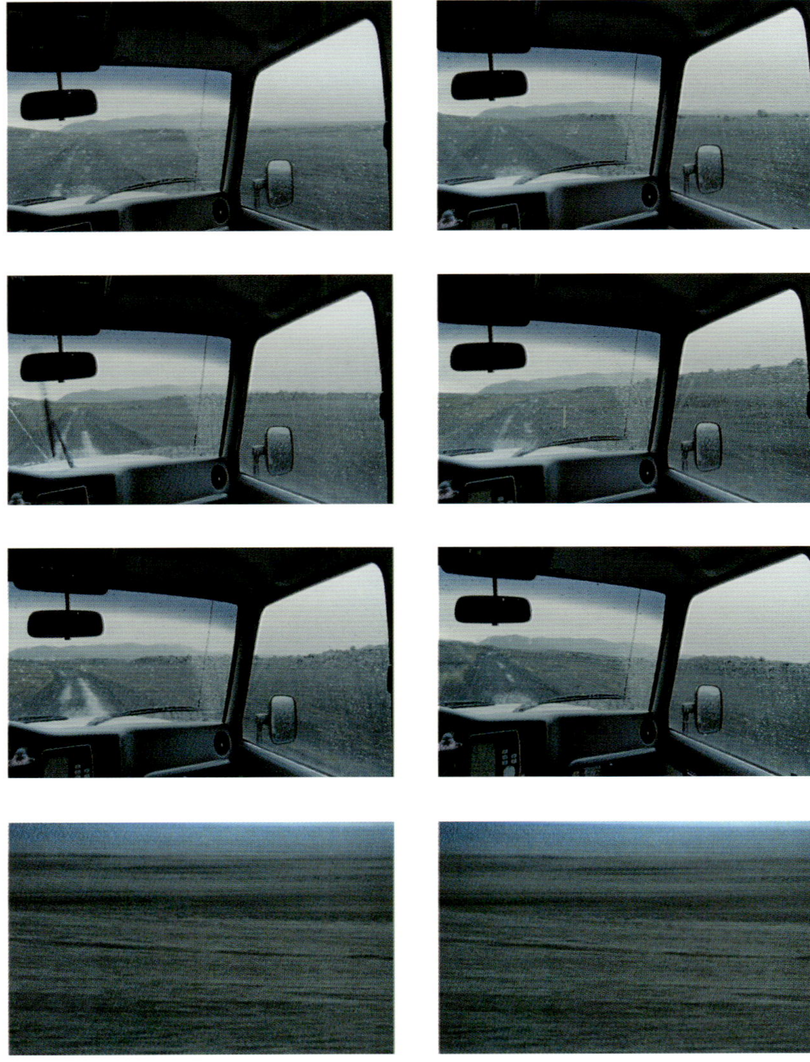

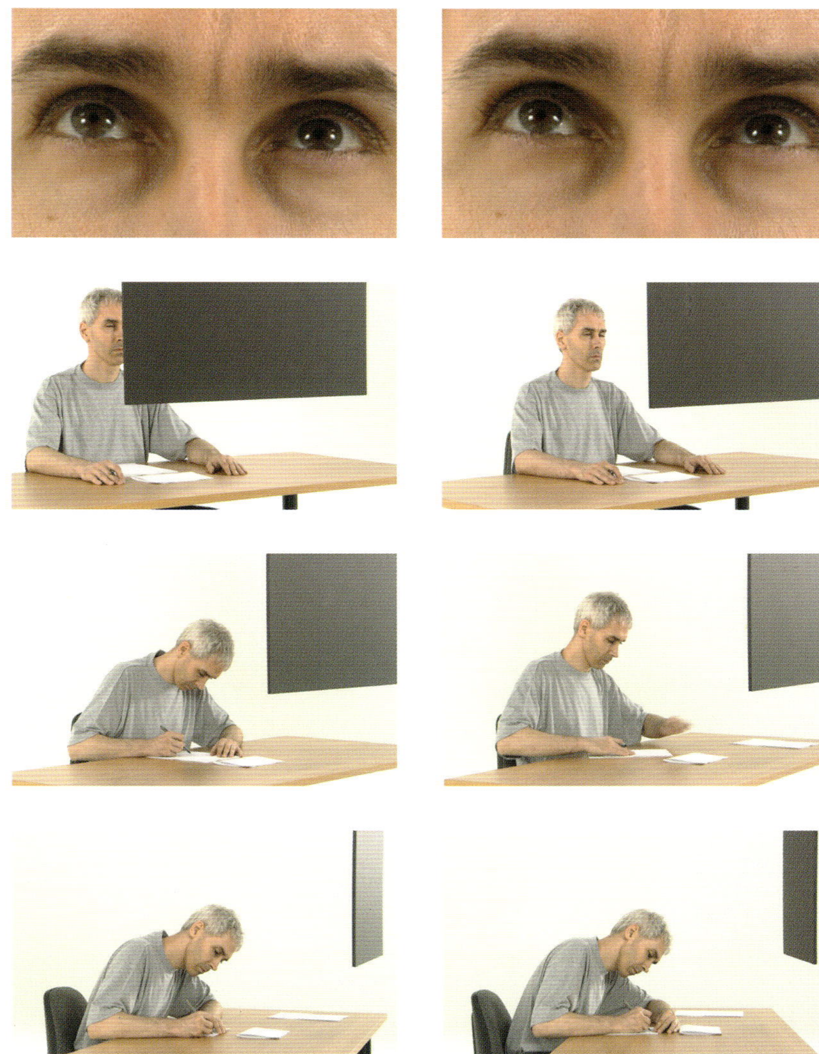

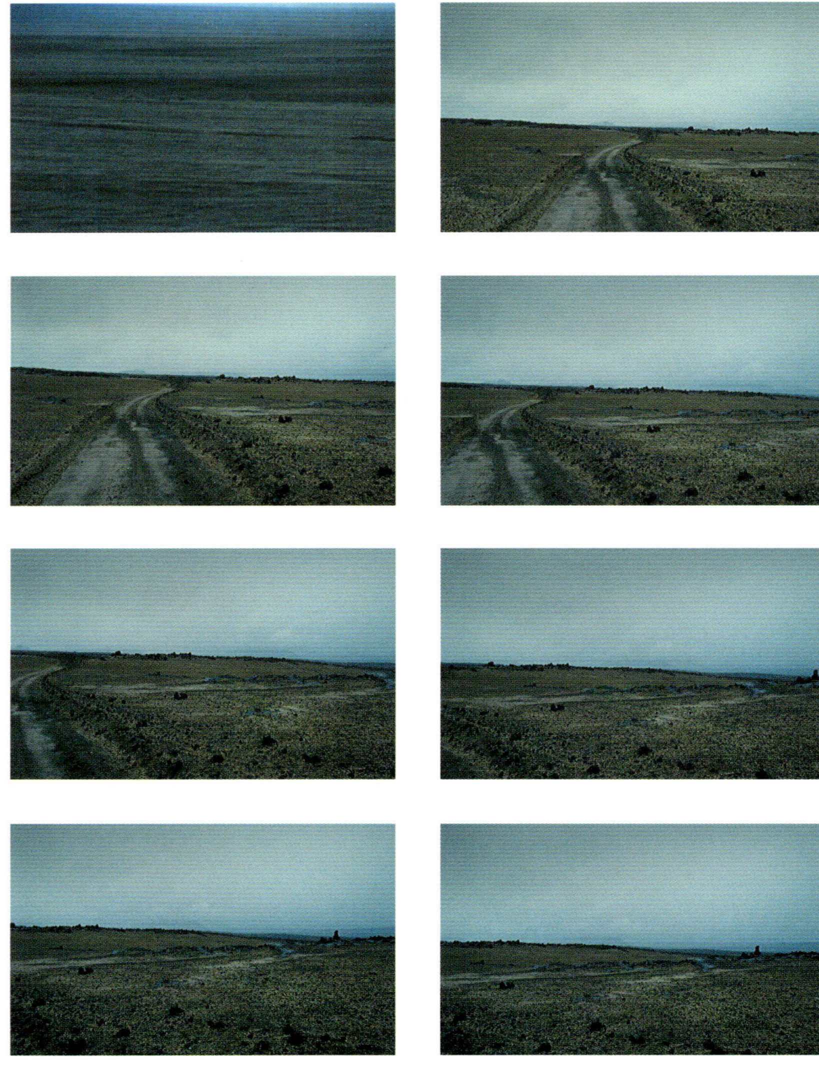

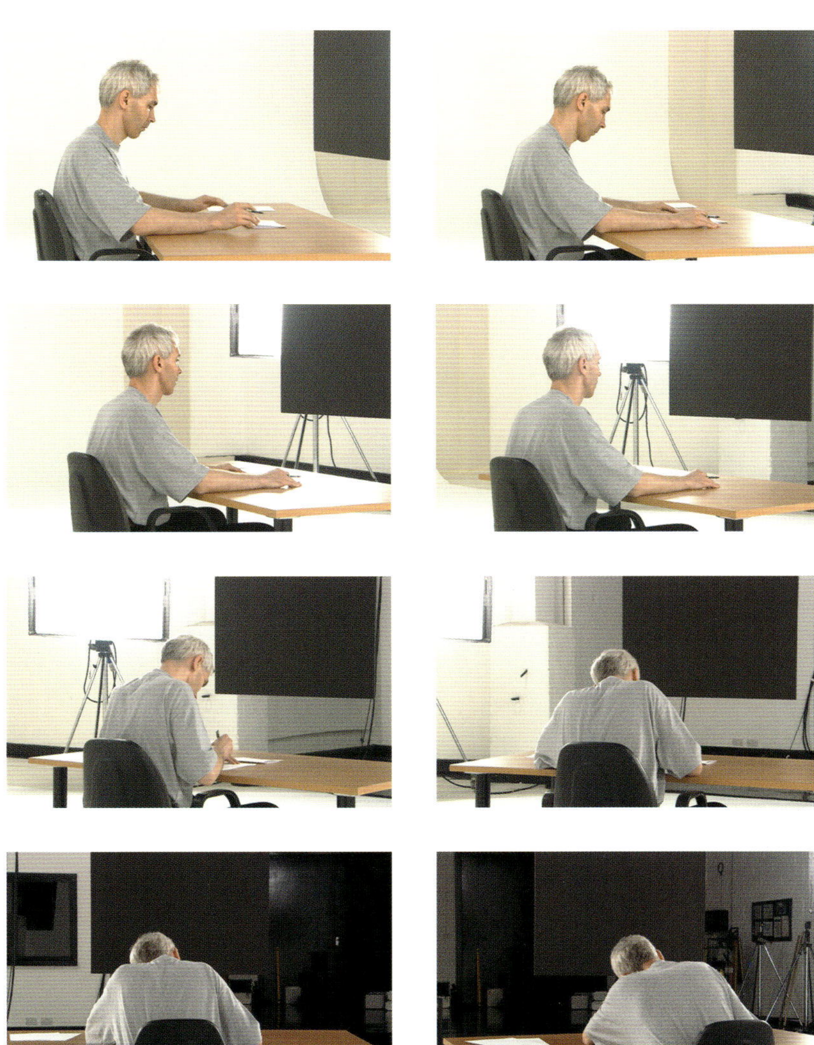

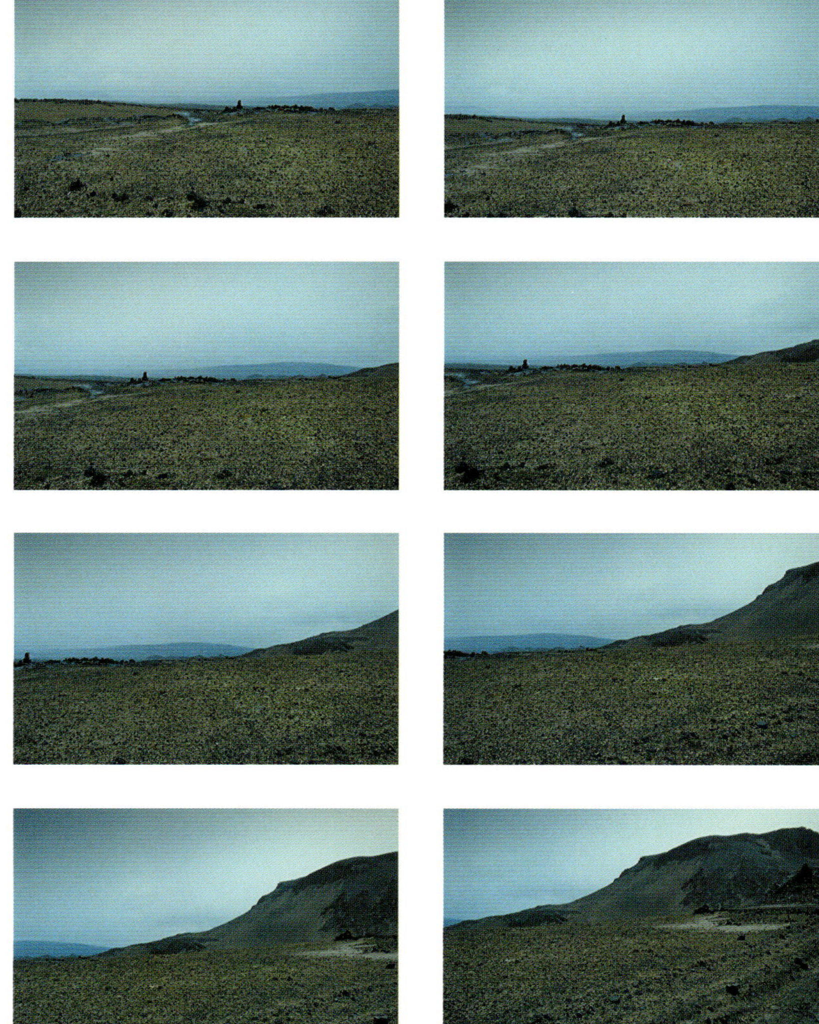

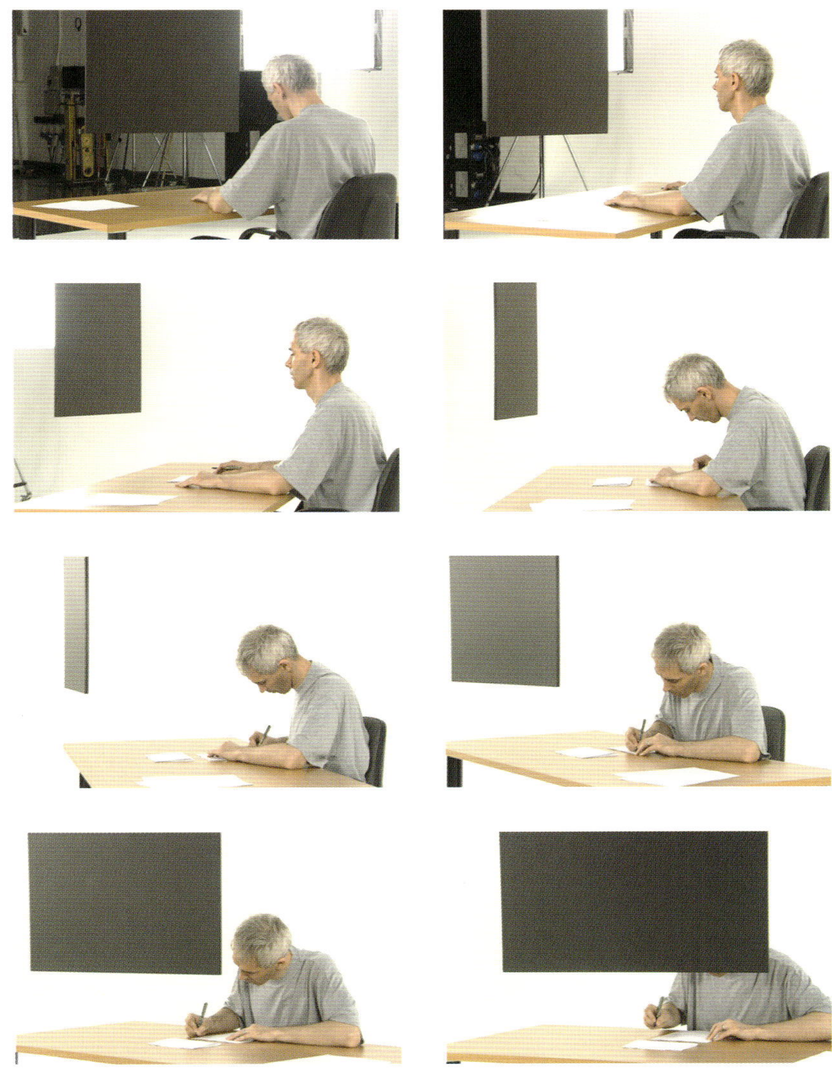

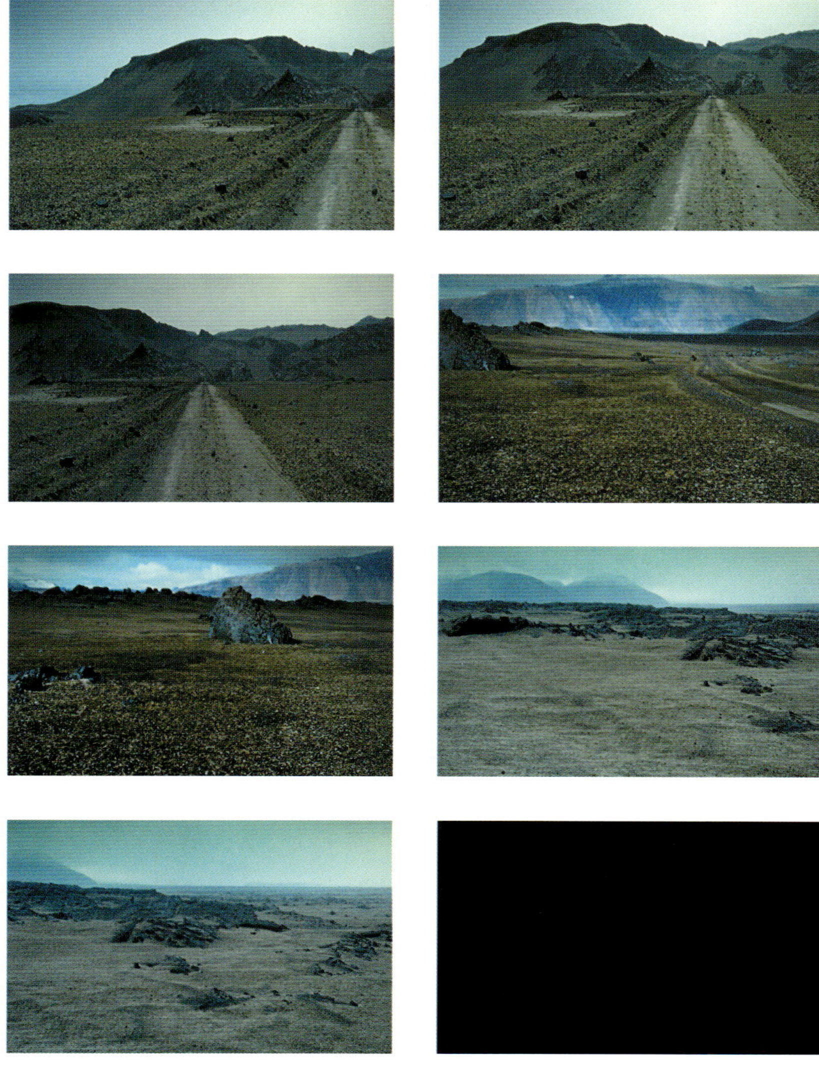

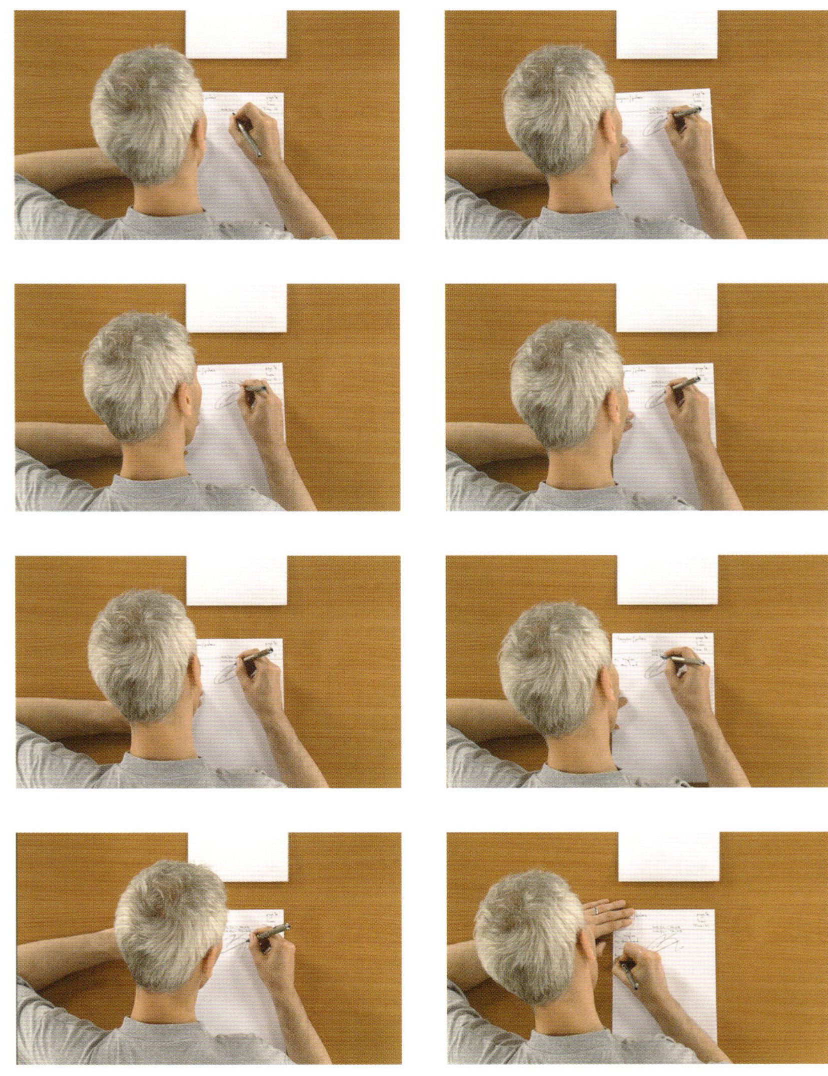

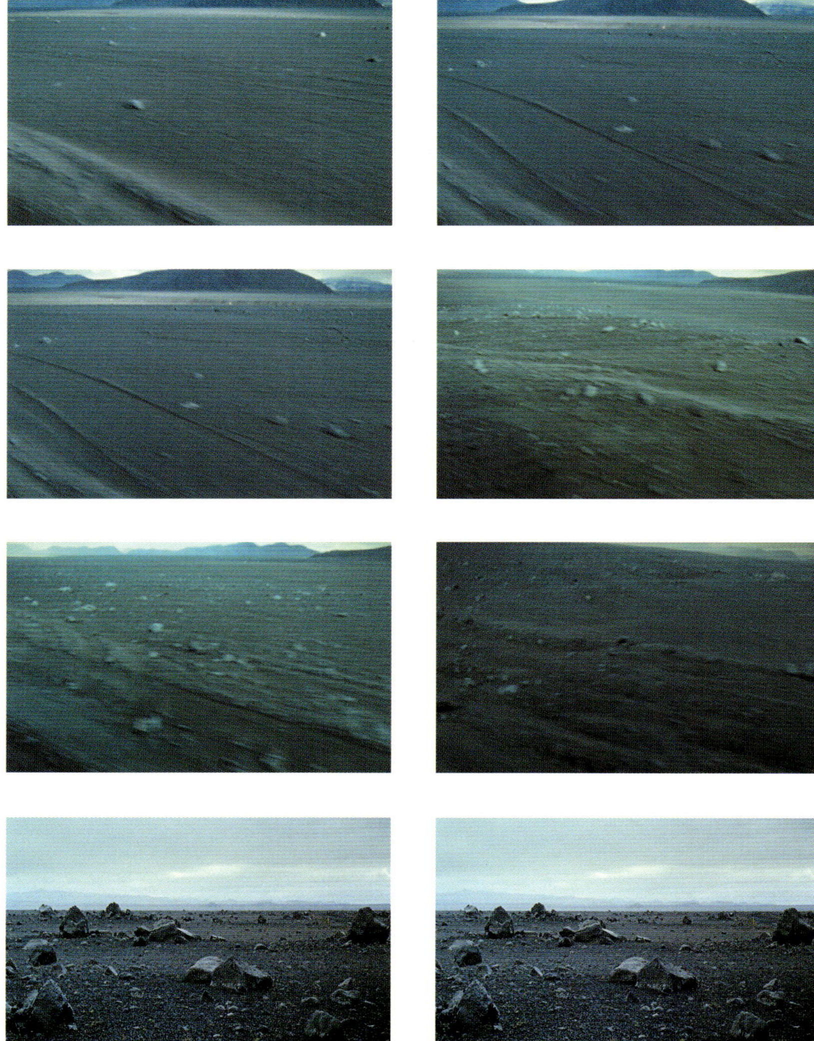

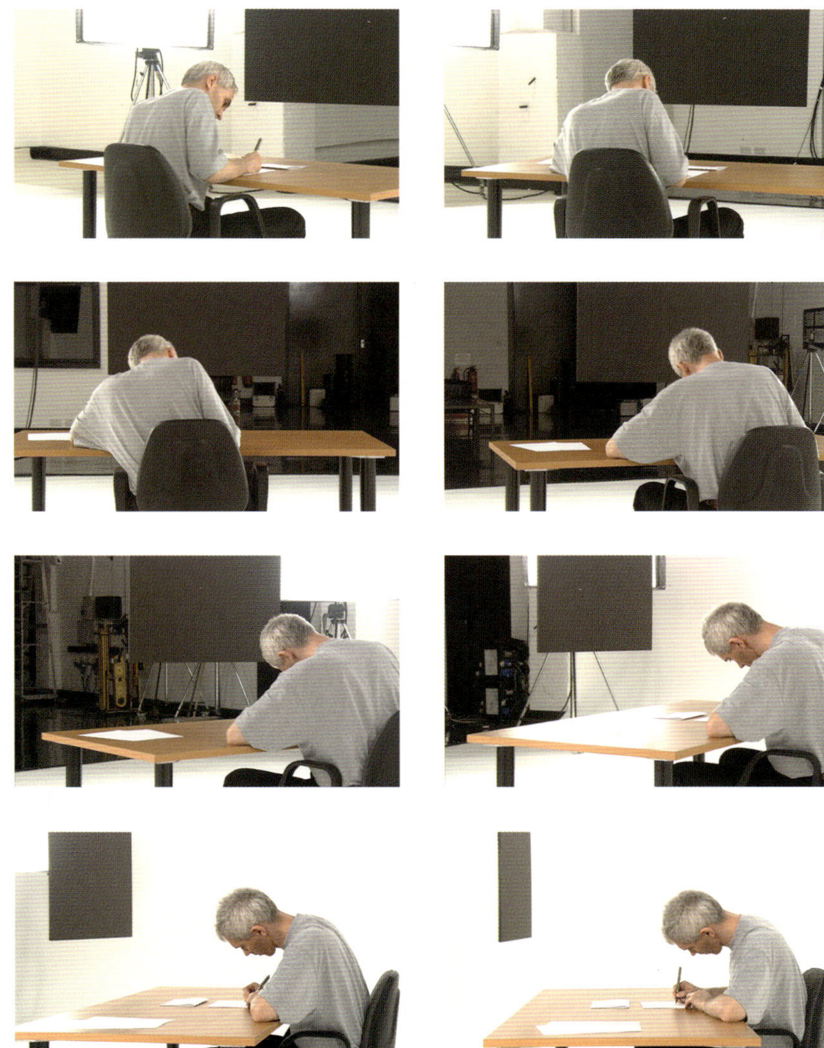

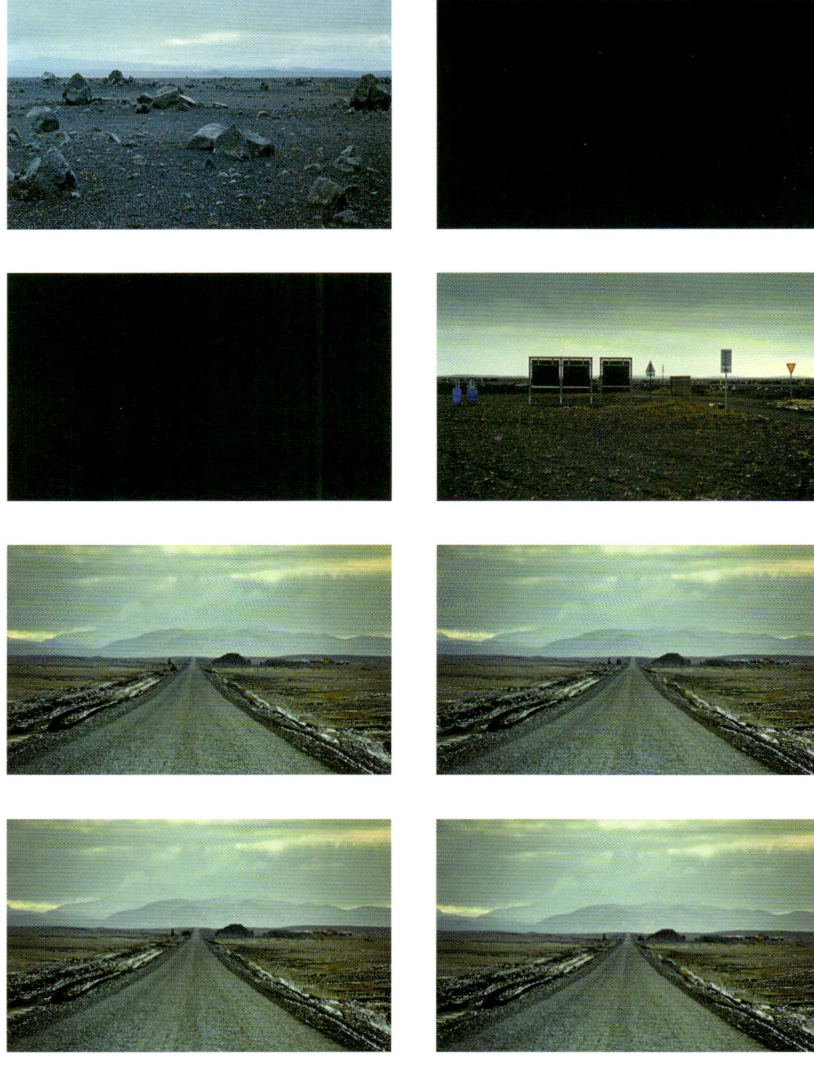

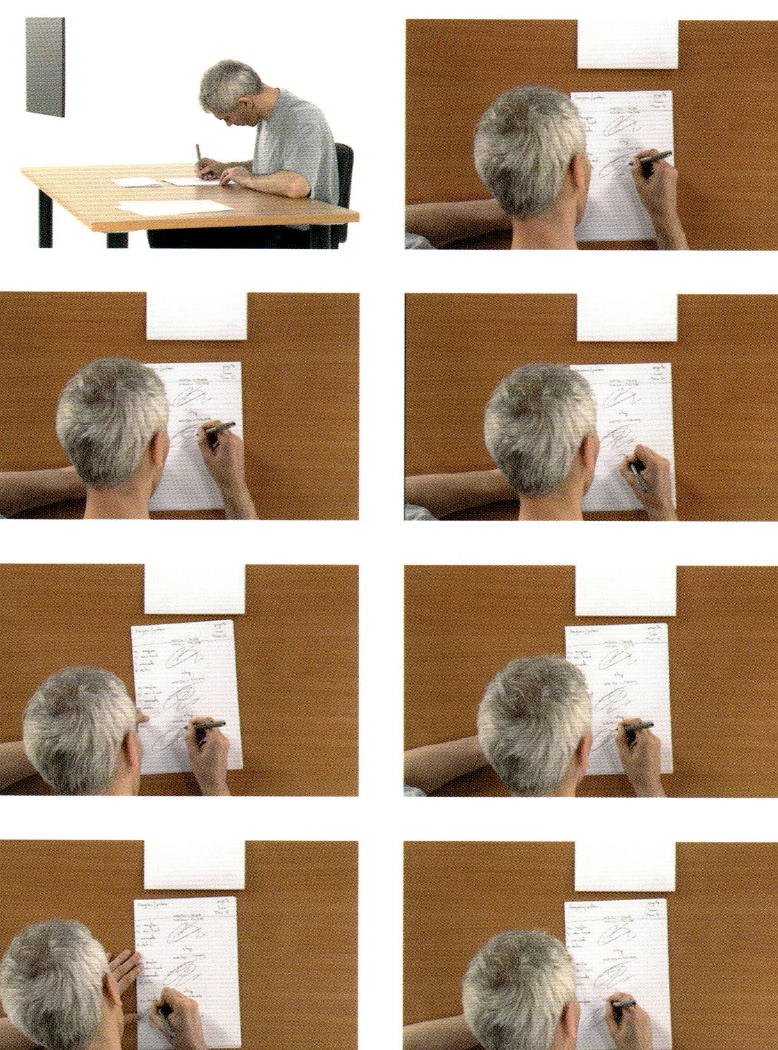

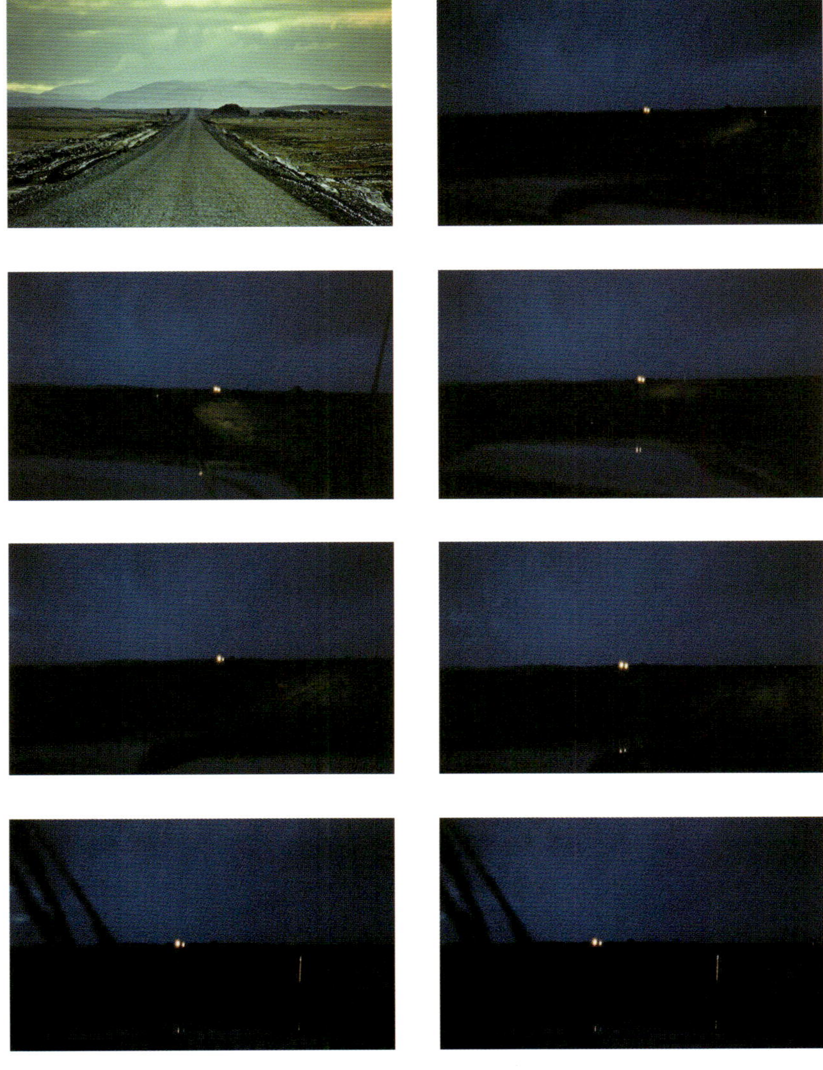

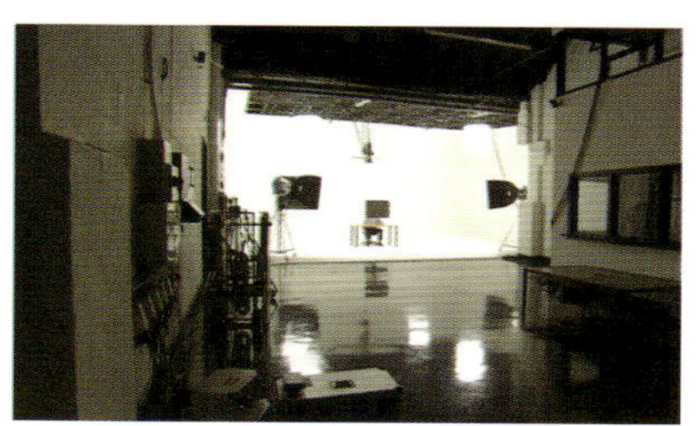
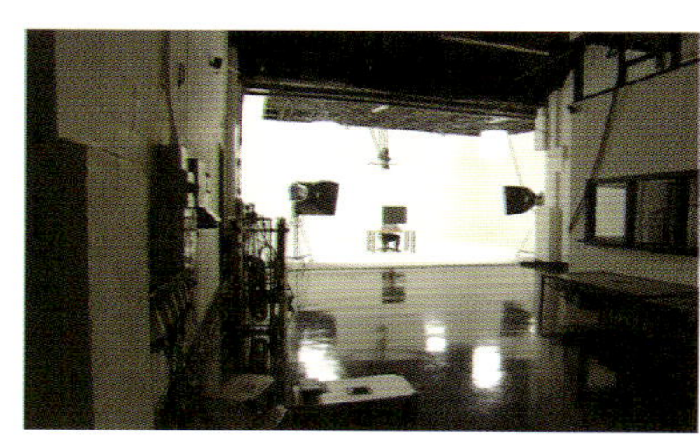
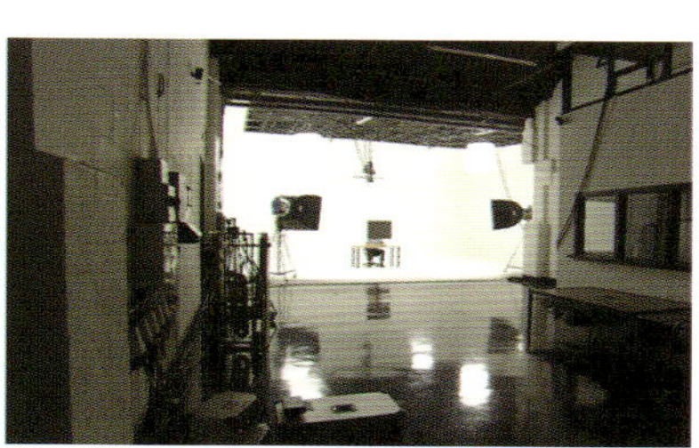
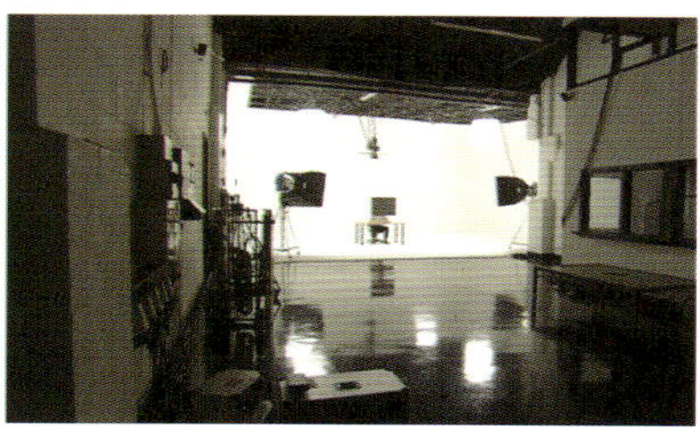
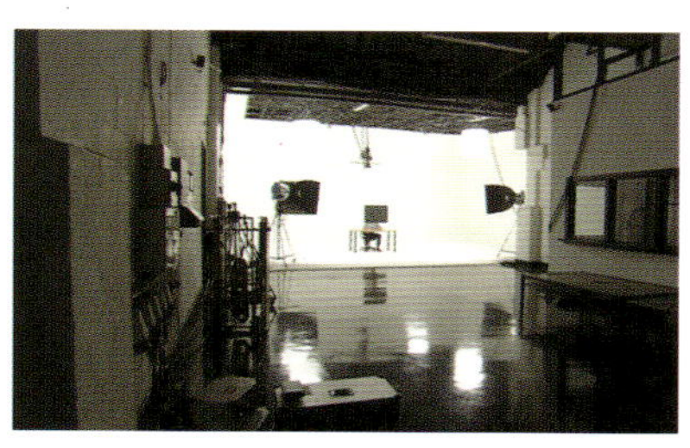
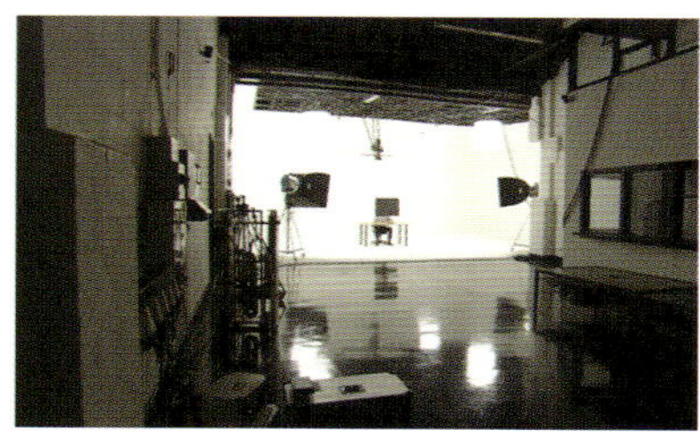
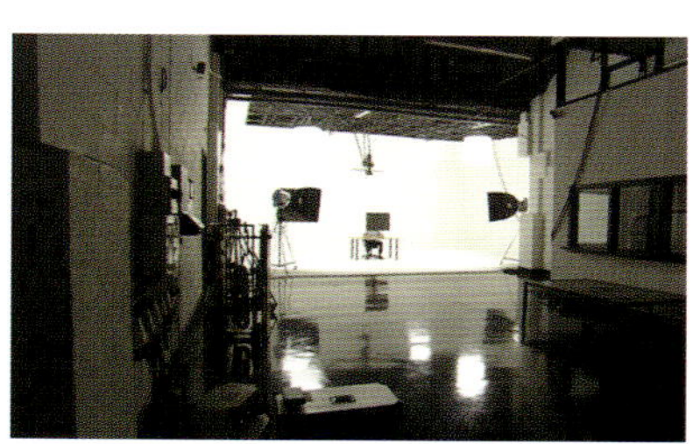
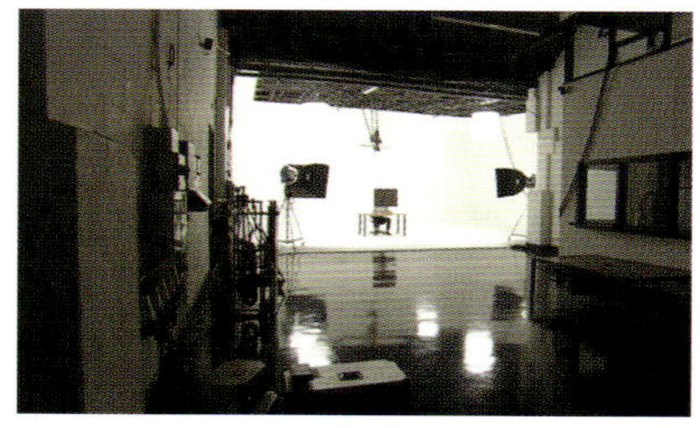

TRANSMISSION
A conversation between Graham Gussin, Steven Bode and Chris Darke

CD: Let's start with the title 'Remote Viewer'. I want you to draw out the elements that are important for you in this title.

GG: The title's been there all along, ever since I saw a documentary about 'remote viewers' about two and a half years ago on TV. It's a very evocative title and it seemed to sum up a lot of the ways I was thinking about location and distance. The title is useful also in that it sets up a kind of role for the viewer — they're included in the title, if you like. I think that scenario is something that happens all the time when we look at art — in a way, we're all 'remote viewers'. There was always this sense that the viewer was actually an operational part of the work.

SB: Graham and I had been talking about doing a piece for some time, but even before the final shape of this work became apparent, the title 'Remote Viewer' was in the air for a while. I thought it was a wonderfully arresting phrase. On the one hand, it captures something of the barren and otherworldly nature of the landscape in which part of the work was set. On the other, it highlights themes of distance and proximity, presence and projection that are part of the terminology of remote viewing but which could apply just as equally to aspects of everyday perception.

CD: Tell me what a 'remote viewer' does.

GG: When you go into the exhibition there's a text on the wall that tells you this. It reads: "A remote viewer is a person trained to focus and hold his or her sub-conscious mind on a distant target that is normally shielded by time and space and record information about that distant person, place or event." There are different methods – or protocols – that are used. Much of the science of remote viewing was developed by the CIA during the Cold War. They would use remote viewers as spies — and they would 'come back' with very detailed descriptions of events and locations. The FBI has also used them to trace kidnap victims. So they're kind of used like an outreach sensing device. I've never met the remote viewer we used in this piece and he's never met me.

CD: Was this one of the conditions of the work?

GG: It was something I decided would be good for the work, to maintain that distance. I felt that if we'd met and talked beforehand he'd know too much. It seemed a good discipline for the piece.

SB: Since Graham wanted to keep that measure of distance, it was left to us at Film and Video Umbrella to find a remote viewer to participate in the work. Although remote viewing is a widely acknowledged and practiced phenomenon in the United States, it isn't nearly as well-known in the UK. We conducted a series of searches on the Internet, and took soundings from the Institute of Psychical Research, the Koestler Foundation and other British parapsychological organisations, but it was a long time until we found the remote viewer, Lee Heather, who agreed to appear in the work.

CD: The question that follows directly from that is how on earth do you audition a remote viewer?

SB: There were a number of things we didn't want to reveal for fear of giving too much away: who we were, who the artist was or what kind of thing we were up to. But at the same time we needed to find out as much as possible about the remote viewer himself. The piece that Graham wanted to make involved a fairly large-scale logistical exercise in which a number of things had to happen simultaneously on the day. We wanted to get an idea of how reliable our remote viewer would be; to be sure that they would turn up, that they would take the project as seriously as us.

CD: It seems that part of the work has to do with creating parameters — for the journey in Iceland and for the remote viewer's activities in London. Can you talk about the specific aspects of those parameters?

GG: The idea was that I would be travelling across Iceland over a period of days with Askja as the final destination. We wanted to key in certain points of time where myself, my cameraman and our guide in Iceland would be completely aware of what was going on in London. We knew that, within a given time-bracket, the remote viewer would be sitting at a table in London attempting to locate me, to see through my own eyes, in a way. It was like having someone looking over my shoulder for that period of time. So, I'd be travelling or looking at the landscape and it was like being a channel or a communications device. We used a number of formal devices to underline this sense of simultaneity: for example, as the camera would be circling the remote viewer in London in a 360 degree tracking shot, we would be in the middle of the desert in Askja doing a 360 degree panning shot on a tripod.

After the shoot, as I started shaping and editing the material, a notion of these things not coinciding directly or just drifting apart from each other became more interesting because the piece isn't about precision. It's not about whether at the end of his two 45-minute sessions, the remote viewer can write down 'Askja' as a bull's-eye. The piece involves a proposition and a relationship between things that is sometimes in focus and sometimes out of focus and seems to shift out of light and dark according to the remote viewer's vision and our opening the shutter on the camera. So, at the end of the edit, we ended up with two different lengths of DVD, with the Iceland footage on one and the London footage on the other. The London footage is slightly longer, so while the two loops start off from the same point they begin to drift throughout the day. I like that because, at certain points, there seem to be definite relationships between the shots. At other times that seems to disappear, or to relax. I like the idea that we're not choreographing the piece and trying to prove something. We're setting up a proposition and allowing the material to behave as it will.

SB: Yes, so while it's true that there was a timetable, a schedule, a series of markers, both formal and geographical, that we would adhere to, all these elements were put in place in order to conduct an experiment. It was interesting how the precise set of conditions we defined for the work was echoed somehow in the equally meticulous procedures of Lee's remote viewing sessions. Although remote viewing revolves around the idea of the viewer projecting himself into another place, it also involves a great deal of notation; of drawing, writing and transcribing onto paper. At certain points, Lee would draw, you could even say 'materialise', a little pictogram. He'd then use his pen almost like a divining-rod, as if to decode or decipher the information contained within it. He was very keen to stress that there is a very precise set of protocols that needs to be gone through to decipher this information. It's a kind of intellectual process as well as something more unquantifiable.

GG: ... they talk about it very much as an innate ability in us all that just takes training to key into... I also like the way that it links in to very popular stuff like holiday brochures and the Internet. I love that sense that we do this all the time, we do have this remote sense of the world. The hotel room or the website is waiting for you and you project yourself into that, receive information back from it and make your decision.

CD: What happens in 'Remote Viewer', it seems to me, is the representation of an act you can't see. It is an act that is not available to sight. You're only seeing the marks and surface traces the remote viewer leaves on the paper. You're not seeing the surface trace he's leaving on his projection blackboard but you are seeing the surface trace on his face when he's concentrating, shutting his eyes and transporting himself. Likewise, on the other screen, you're seeing the surface traces left on the landscape around Askja.

GG: There was a moment, and perhaps I was foolish not to have seen this right from the beginning, when I was editing the work and looking at the two projection screens and I suddenly sat back in my chair and said 'There's nothing to see!' The information is not in the footage at all. The information is purely in the possible relationship or the proposition which this sets up. It's like the inert gas pieces by Robert Barry where he goes into the desert, releases some inert gas and takes a photograph of it. There's nothing to see. But somehow he's impregnated that image with an idea, with a proposition; with an idea about dissipation and a question about what is visual. That's what I was hoping 'Remote Viewer' would do and I suddenly realised that it was operating like that because there was nothing to see. It was in the air between these two screens, not on the screen.

SB: In a way, the fact that there is 'nothing to see' frees up the mind to project, to discover relationships. Such as in the two parallel circling tracking shots. I'd seen them right from the very beginning as being like traces of the invisible orbits of radar and satellites, a possible call-and-response between invisible force-fields that were trying to locate each other and didn't know what they were looking for. They have a lovely symmetry and a lot of this work is about symmetry; although it's also about chance, about coincidence, about synchronicity.

GG: I feel that if the work had been more choreographed, if each shot had been locked in to each other shot, I'd have been making a more fictional piece of work. The links between the images would have become overriding whereas I'm just as interested in the spaces and the differences between the images as I am in the similarities or coincidences between them. Maybe it doesn't add up. Maybe the space between these two things is immense and it doesn't work ...

CD: It's interesting that in the process of editing you realised that there was nothing to see. In a way that's a sign that a certain number of steps in the production had actually been successful. Tell me whether that discovery inflected your decision about how to install the work.

GG: I think not. The point when I understood the way that this work should be installed was really coming back from Iceland and seeing the footage. I wasn't present at the London shoot. I knew it was taking place, of course, but I had no idea how it would feel. When I saw the London footage it became very clear to me that what we needed to do was transport that studio environment into the piece somehow; that that white non-background background needed to be in the piece. It was so evocative and perfect for the work because those studio backgrounds, after all, are used to take photographs of things that can then be 'transported' to other places. A photograph of a car will be taken in the studio, and then matted together with a photograph of a far-off landscape. The piece involves the same idea, one thing against another, one thing being moved out of its position and being transported to another place. I thought it would be fantastic if we could use the physicality of that phenomenon and bring it right into the piece. Again, as soon as I saw the black screen that Lee uses as a projection device hanging in front of the table in the studio, it seemed to say 'that's the stuff that the installation is made of.' It also became apparent that the two screens should be facing each other rather than being side-by-side. Each screen then became a mirror or projection-board of the other. It also made me realise the temporal sense of the work, that it didn't have a beginning and an end.

SB: In the same way as Graham was in Iceland and hadn't seen the London shoot, I was in London and hadn't seen the Iceland footage. So even though Graham can talk about the fact that 'there's nothing to see', it's an incredibly haunting and beautiful kind of nothingness. The landscape around Askja is deep in the interior of Iceland, in a very remote place they call the 'lunar desert'. In the lead-up to the project, Graham had used a quote which described it as 'the nearest faraway place'. Apart from being somewhere which is literally in the middle of nowhere, it also has a certain history in that NASA had taken the US astronauts there to train them, not only for its physical resemblance to the lunar landscape but in terms of them adjusting to a place with hardly any frame-of-reference.

GG: They talked about it as being a kind of psychological preparation because the astronauts were surrounded constantly day and night and they felt that they needed to take them out of that environment and prepare them for the shock of going to a place where there really was no trace of humankind whatsoever. They were worried that there might be some psychological reaction to that which wasn't foreseen...

CD: I think there's an element within the piece that's worth exploring from the point of view of the contemporary political moment. It touches on what's a fairly well-developed discourse about military technology and perception that departs from Virilio. You've already mentioned NASA, the CIA and the FBI. In some way you're taking on technology, whether it's human technology embodied in the shape of the remote viewer, or in the shape of Askja and its place in the history of the moon landings. There is a level at which this work sits alongside discourses about the militarisation of perception.

GG: I think that the ways these technologies can be and are employed by governments and corporations are frightening and overwhelming. But sometimes you can invert or subvert or critique that simply by removing it from its enforced operative status in the world. We're not employing the remote viewer or his apparatus, if you like, to undermine, threaten or trespass. We're undoing it, deconstructing it, thinking about where this process might lead to; whether it's a facility we all have, whether it's something that we use every day. You could compare it with how we think about art, for example. A lot of people on the outside think contemporary art is outlandish, unnecessary and for cranks. There's a kind of paranoia about it. But then again there are people on the inside who are practicing and thinking about it and who think it's incredibly worthwhile and that it's a facility that everyone else has. In a way, I think it has something to do with cultural practice and hopefully it's understanding and encouraging of that cultural practice and of the alternatives available.

CD: Tell me more about the protocol the remote viewer used to locate his target.

SB: At the start of each of the two sessions, I had to write down on a piece of paper the name of the subject – Graham Gussin – the name of the location – Askja – and the time – which was the present time. After I had written this down, I then had to write two groups of four letters which I could choose entirely at random. As I was writing them I was asked to think of the subject, the location and the time in which it was happening, so as to make a mental link with the letters I was writing. I then had to write the letters on a separate sheet of paper and hand that sheet to Lee. This tiny fragment of information was all that he would then have to decode. But the fact that I was asked to visualise where Graham was and make a mental link between the location and the letters I was writing brought in a lot of interesting things for me in the possible overlap between remote viewing and mind-reading.

GG: There are different methods that different remote viewers use. Some go into more trance-like states and recall their experiences afterwards. Others sit down with a piece of paper and write out tables and diagrams. Others visit a place to soak up the atmosphere and recall an incident that's happened there.

CD: Are you employing this particular kind of activity of remote viewing to question your and our necessary credulity? Or is it something that allows you to set up a parallel proposition? Because it strikes me, to repeat something that you said at the top of this conversation, that the remote viewer is also the spectator; that the remote viewer is there as a kind of surrogate for the spectator.

GG: It's very much the subject of the work. That the notion of credulity, or you could use the word 'trust', is inherent and intrinsic to looking at art, to immersing yourself in something and allowing it to have its effect. That's very much to do with trust — there's a kind of invitation, there's a space for the viewer. It wouldn't work without that space. At the same time, there's the implication that 'if you trust me you could well be in danger, you could well be in danger of having the wool pulled over your eyes, you could well be in danger of being led into a dark place'. I like the kind of tension that's produced within the viewer, because that's the place where questions get asked.

CD: I wonder if there's anything you wanted to say about the relationship between landscape and 'the sublime' and its modification by technology?

GG: It has bearings on my practice generally, this notion of the sublime and what it is that goes to make up that vision. I have been trying to explore this in a number of pieces using sound and images, trying to get at the mechanism of that notion of the sublime; to deconstruct it, if you like. I do think it's there in 'Remote Viewer' and, as you say, whenever you talk about landscape it's a difficult thing to get away from. I think it's there in the sense of scale that's involved and the sense of being at a distance from something — the desire to project into that but also the safe distance we maintain which is very much part of the way that the notion of the sublime works.

SB: ... that parallel and simultaneous sense of 'beauty and terror'. The idea of both being present and lost in a landscape at the same time.

GG: I wanted the use of scale to be strong in this piece, using sound along with the images to achieve this, to have a changing relationship between the sense of near and far. The only sound in the piece is that of the viewer drawing and breathing, very close-up, almost internal noises. This sound with the wide-open landscape is crucial. It's hallucinogenic, this exchange; a co-habitation of micro and macro worlds.

CD: When it comes up for discussion concerning landscape, I wonder if 'the sublime' provides a way around the idea that Walter Benjamin expressed in his essay 'The Work of Art in the Age of Mechanical Reproduction'. Namely, with the advent of the technologically reproduced image, that the 'aura' is no longer possible. We've lived with such images for over one hundred years now. Could it be that the idea of the 'aura' becomes re-located to the notion of 'the sublime' as it attaches to technological reproductions of landscape?

GG: Not just of landscape but with all images.

SB: Benjamin's idea was that the particular aura of the unique object becomes increasingly eroded by its constant reproduction, but it's true that there are certain types of images which seem to resist that, where something persists. It's interesting that the word 'aura' has this specific art-historical meaning but that it also has another, extra-sensory, resonance. There's the idea, for instance, that we all have 'auras' which are invisible but which can be detected by 'sensitive' individuals. On one level, this can all come across as pretty far-fetched. But on another it can provide a useful metaphor for how we look at art. How the visible is only one part of the spectrum, if you like. How, on occasions, there can be 'nothing to see', but how that nothing can be incredibly charged. I like the way that 'Remote Viewer', while apparently evoking these otherworldly, extra-sensory powers, actually reminds us of ideas and experiences we encounter every day.

London, April 2002

STEVEN BODE IS DIRECTOR OF FILM AND VIDEO UMBRELLA
CHRIS DARKE IS A WRITER AND CRITIC

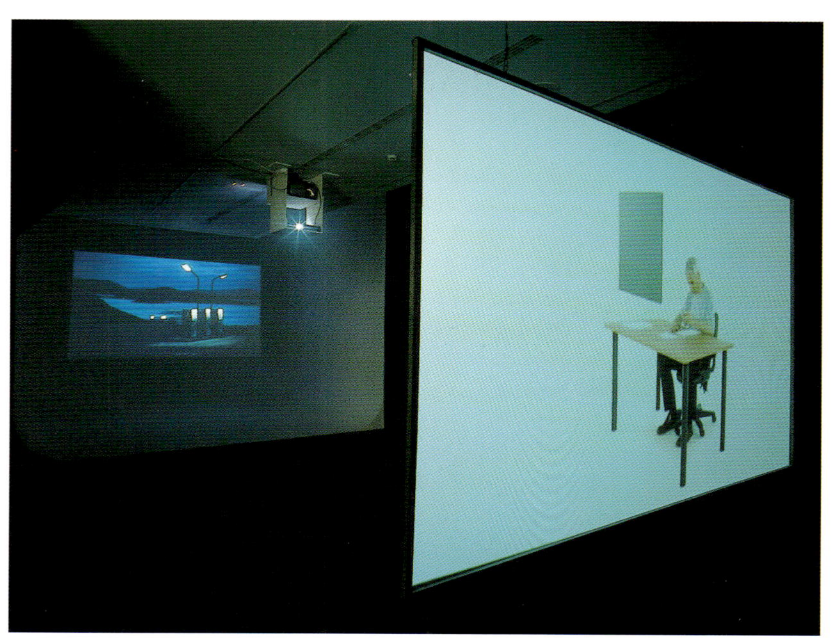

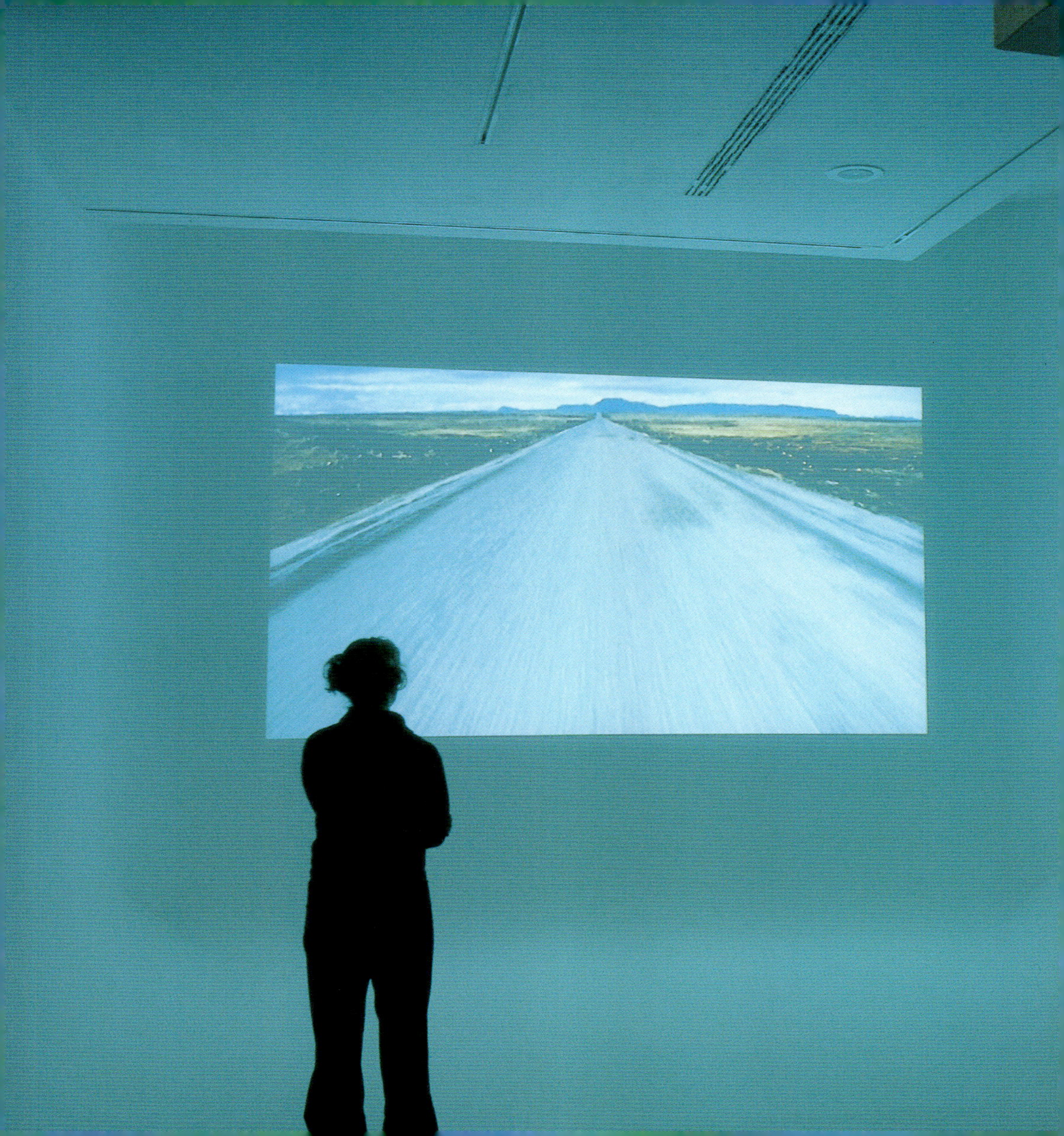

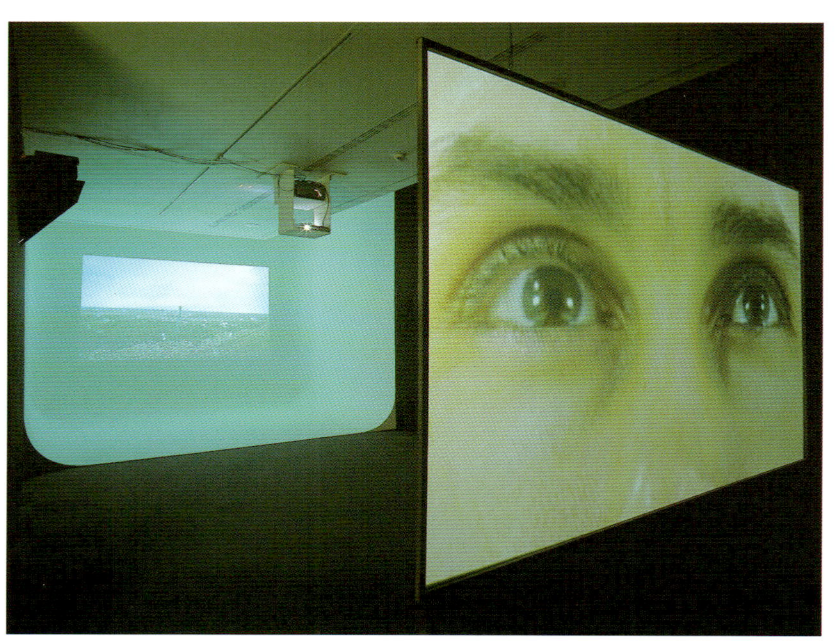

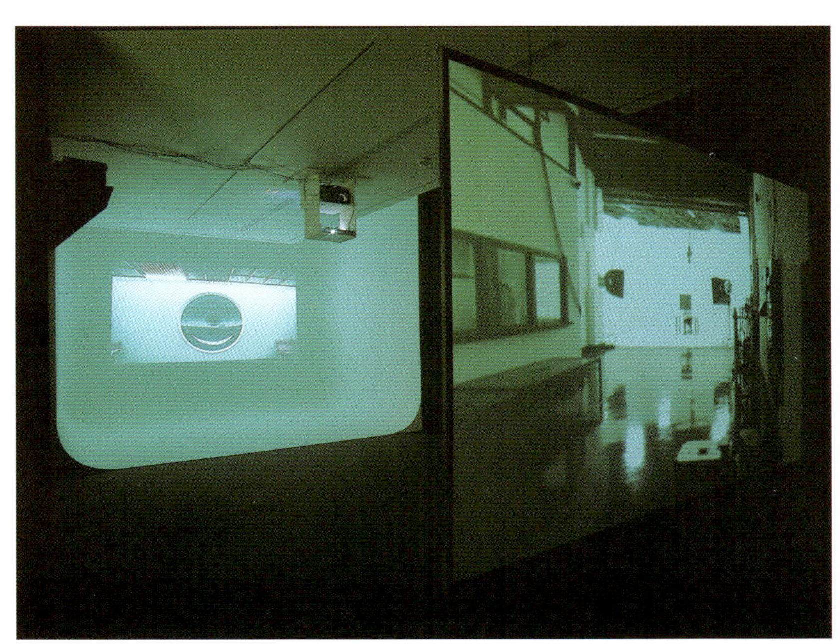

ideogram / probes

page 1A:
Lee:
Time: H

MRJO — TMSB

MRJO — TMSB

PL: simplex
B: semi-hard
I: manmade
A: static

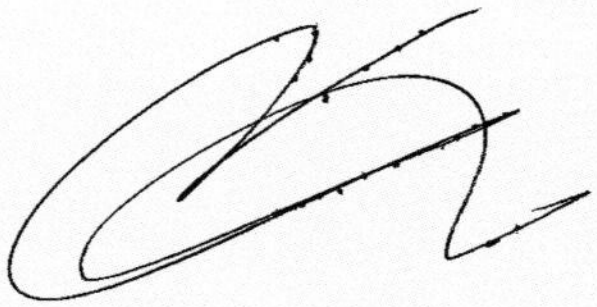

stop

MRJO — TMSB

PL: simplex
B: semi-hard
I: manmade
A: static

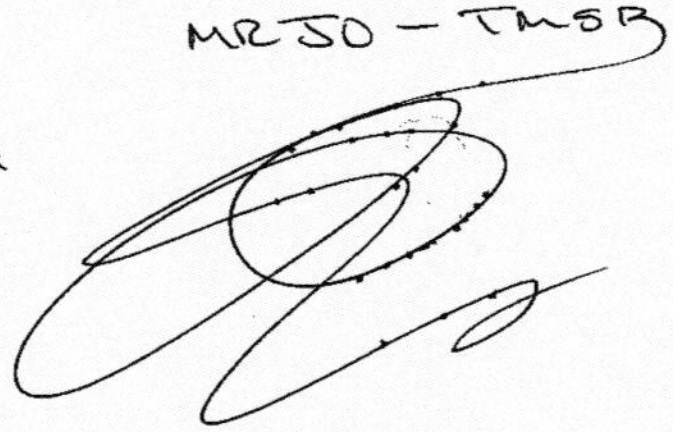

stop

MRJO — TMSB

PL: simplex
B: semi-hard
I: manmade
A: static

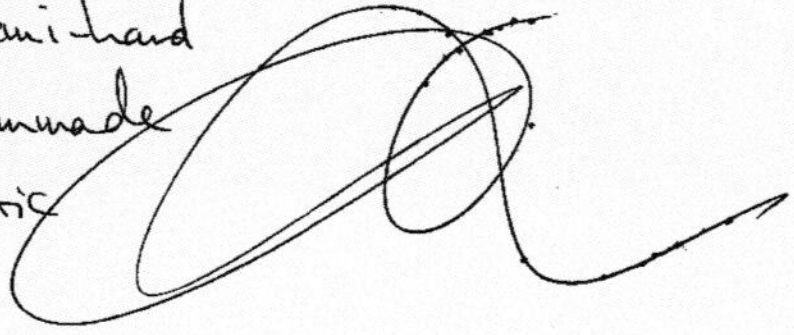

stop

ideogram

Lee:

MRJO — TMSB
MRJO — TMSB

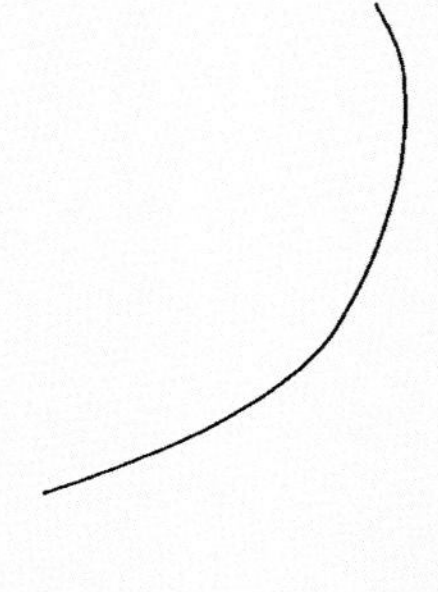

ideogram

MRJO — TMSB
MRJO — TMSB

stop

ideogram/probes

KSGL-RRBV

KSGL-RRBV

PL: complex
B: semi-soft
I: manmade
A: static

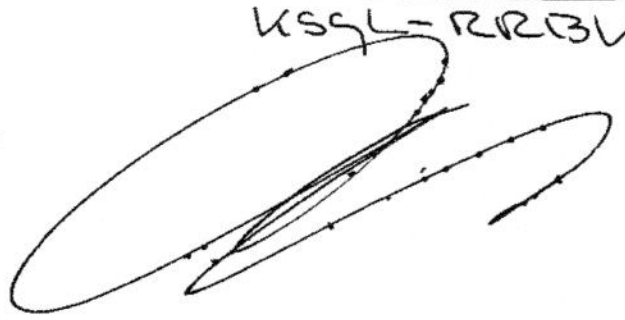

stop

PL: complex
D: semi-soft
I: natural
A: static

KSGL-RRBV

stop

PL: complex
B: semi-soft
I: natural
A: static

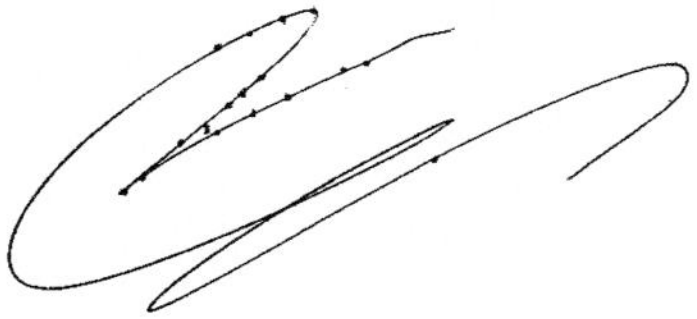

KSGL-RRBV

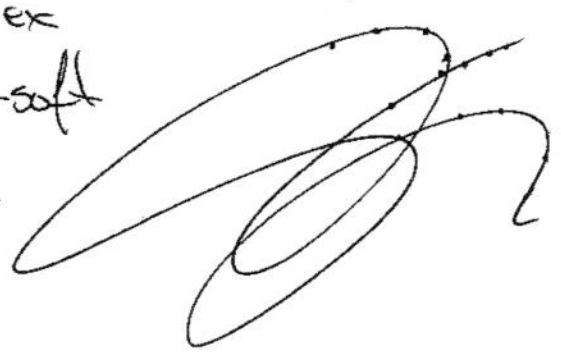

stop

Cascade

Land _1_   Air __   Water __   Energy —

Structure _1_   Obstacle ____

Life: veg _low_
Life: human _multiple_
Life: other _

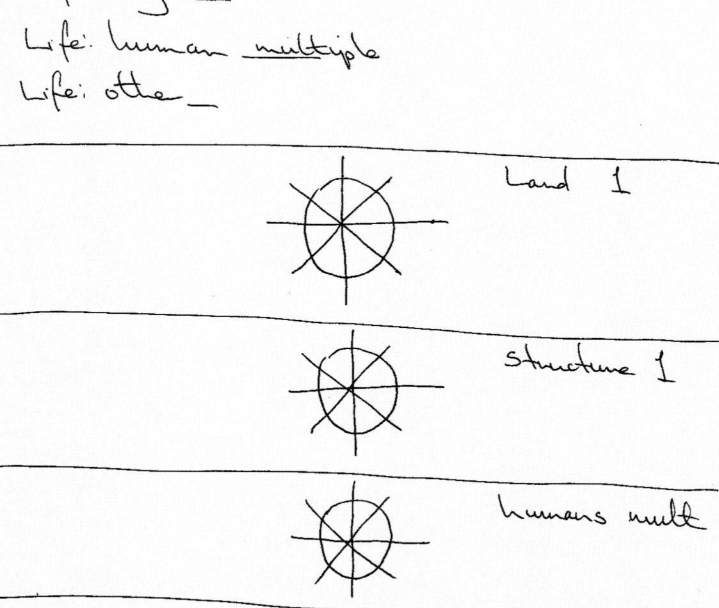

Blackboard   Land 1

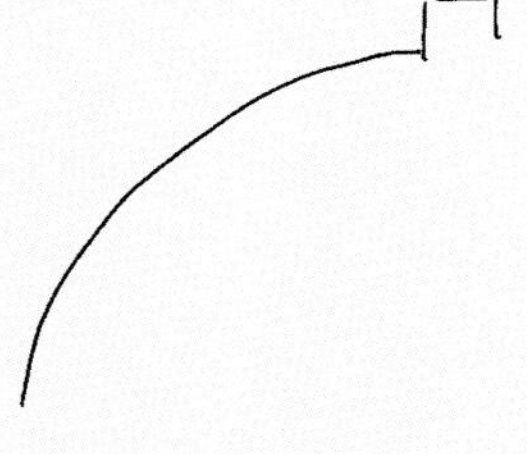

stop

graham gussin/askja/present time

MRJO — TMSB

graham gussin/askja/present time

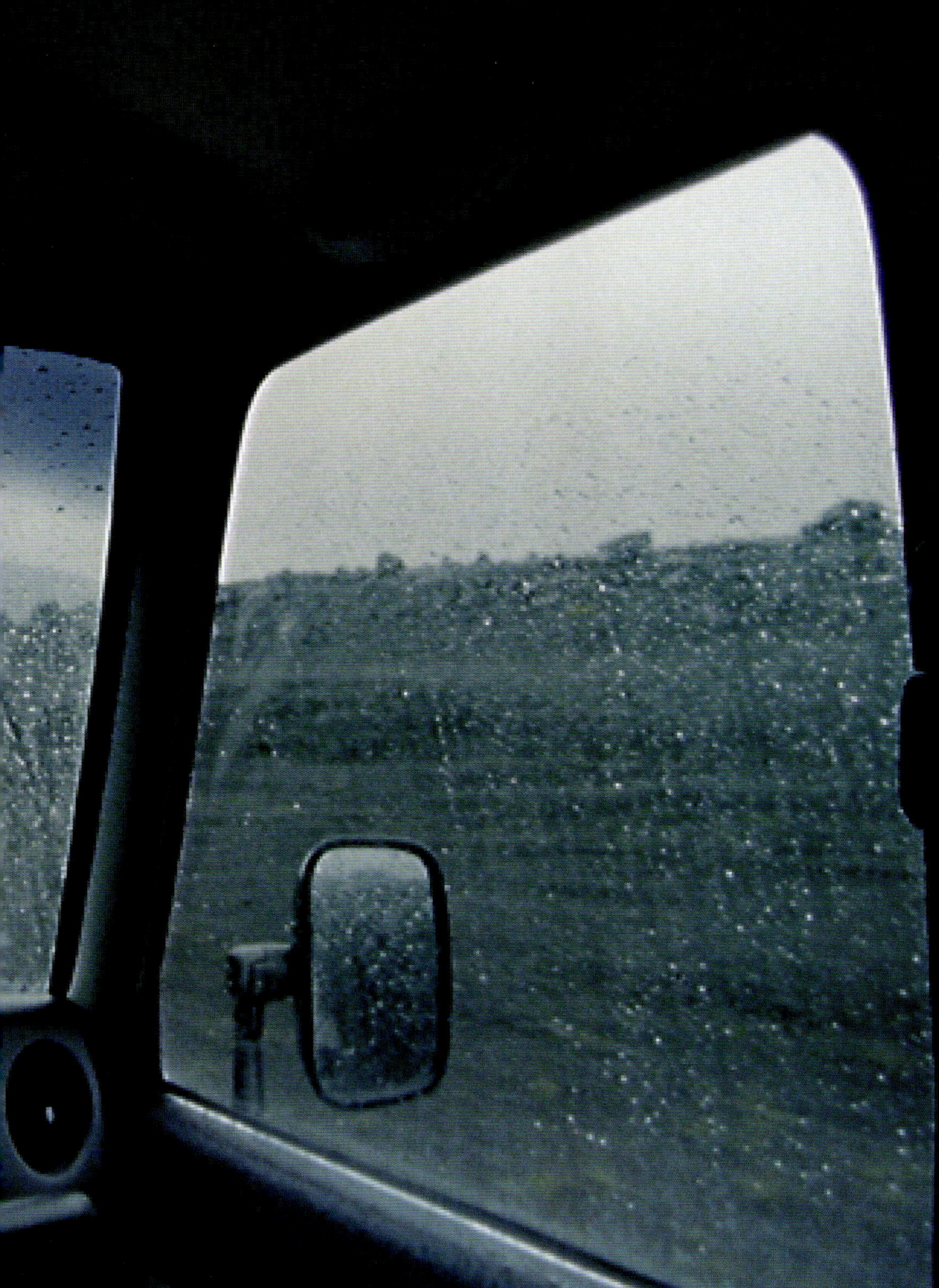

GRAHAM GUSSIN: REMOTE VIEWER

Published by Film and Video Umbrella
Edited by Steven Bode
Designed by Secondary Modern, with thanks to
MarMarCo
Printed by Trichrom Ltd

Published to accompany the Film and Video
Umbrella touring exhibition, 'Remote Viewer'
by Graham Gussin, commissioned by Film and
Video Umbrella and Ikon Gallery.
With additional support from the
Henry Moore Foundation.

Publication supported by the National Touring
Programme of the Arts Council of England.
With additional support from East England
Arts and Chelsea School of Art/The London
Institute.

The artist would like to thank:
Steven Bode, Mike Jones, Bevis Bowden,
Caroline Smith, Keith Whittle, Nina Ernst and
Judith Glynne at Film and Video Umbrella,
Jonathan Watkins and Kaye Winwood at Ikon
Gallery.

Printed in an edition of 1,000

ISBN 0-9538634-9-2

© 2002, Film and Video Umbrella, the artist and
the authors

Film and Video Umbrella
52 Bermondsey Street
London SE1 3UD
t 020 7407 7755 f 020 7407 7766
e info@fvu.co.uk   www.fvumbrella.com

Film Credits:

Iceland
Camera: Bevis Bowden
Guide: Gunnar Johannesson at Mountain View
Shot on 16mm film en route from Reykjavik
Airport to Askja, Iceland, 13/14 September
2001
With thanks to Patrick Rolston at
Ice Film Equipment

London
Camera: Martin Testar
Camera Assistant: Mark Cowley
Grip: Rob Barlow
Lighting: Danny Murphy
Production Assistant: Gary Fischer
Remote Viewer: Lee James Heather
Shot on high-definition video at
Holborn Studios, London, 14 September 2001
With thanks to Barry Noakes at
Metro Broadcast

Post Production
Offline: Bevis Bowden
Telecine: George Kyriacou at SVC
DS Operator: Jimmy Honney at Frontline TV
Online: Stephen Murphy at Frontline TV

Installation photographs: Jerry Hardman-Jones

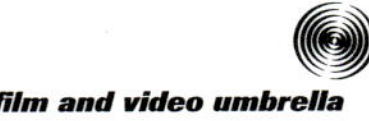

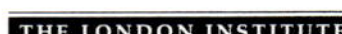

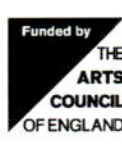

IKON   The Henry Moore Foundation   eastengland|arts